M000087342

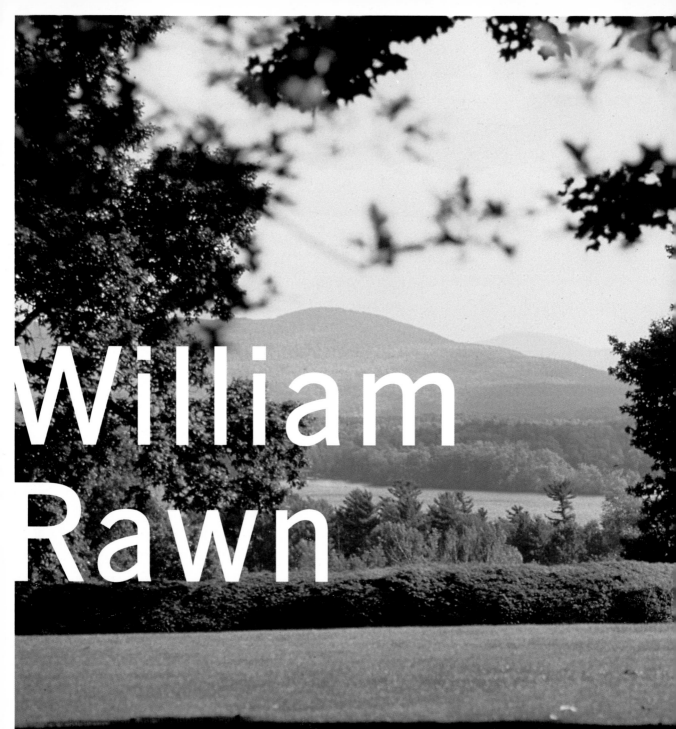

William
Rawn

Architecture For the Public Realm

William Rawn:
Architecture
For the
Public Realm
by Raul A.
Barreneche

William Rawn followed a slightly different path into the design world than most architects. His first calling—though not his true calling—was not architecture, but the law. He completed a degree at Harvard Law School in 1969 and went to work at a private law firm in Washington, D.C. As a practicing attorney he wanted more involvement in the public arena and with the physical environment, interests that led him to the position of Assistant Chancellor for Physical Planning at the University of Massachusetts' Boston campus. After two years as a lawyer and four years as an administrator, Rawn decided to take a turn at design instead. He moved back across the river, this time to the architecture school at MIT.

I remember Bill describing this unorthodox career path (which also included a successful turn as an artist, with work at Pace Gallery in New York City) several years ago, in Washington, coincidentally. I was curious about his professional change of heart, and wondered how the experience had served him as an architect, but he didn't want to dwell on this chapter of his life. He seemed to want to gloss over his whole experience as a lawyer, as if it had no bearing on his current profession. I didn't doubt that he was happy with his second career. In fact, he was enjoying a high point at that moment, receiving great attention in the press as well as prestigious design awards, including national honors from the American Institute of Architects. But I was convinced that a legal foundation, something few architects of his stature can claim on their curriculum vitae, must have had a strong hand in shaping his approach to architecture.

In preparing this book, I've had the chance again to consider the work of William Rawn Associates, and to read Bill's own words describing his architecture and the process that shapes it. It strikes me that the thoroughness with which he thinks about buildings and their settings, and his precise and painstakingly careful analysis of a project, might well be the manifestations of his legal background. Certainly, any good architect preparing for a design commission will dig deep to study a site and research building types. But, perhaps like a lawyer poring over historical records and analyzing precedents, even interviewing witnesses and experts, Rawn demonstrates a particular analytic rigor in his design process. He considers every question possible to cover all his bases, as a legal expert would.

Take for example Rawn's analysis of waterfront cities. In this volume, you will read his ideas about urban waterfronts in his essay "Where the City Meets the Water." This is just a tiny portion, though, of the exhaustive research he has conducted. Rawn has carefully considered the nuances of different bodies of water, such as rivers, harbors, oceans, and canals, and how each affects the character of cities. He has analyzed the ways that water shaped grand cities like London, Paris, and Berlin, as well as smaller, all-American towns such as Charleston, South Carolina; Savannah, Georgia; and his adopted hometown of Boston.

This kind of analysis has helped Rawn define his own attitudes and philosophies about the nature of building in waterfront cities. It has aided him in shaping sensitive master plans, like his urban guidelines for Rochester, New York, which addressed the fact that the city embraced both shores of its river, preserved important panoramic views, and envisioned inhabitable multi-layered bridges. And it has let him create buildings that are sensitive to their waterside contexts, such as the Charlestown Navy Yard townhouses on Boston Harbor, which draw on an exact mix of existing building types on the city's waterfront. Rawn's analysis works across different scales, connecting the building to the city and the city to the building.

Rawn has similarly probed the symbiotic relationships between university campuses and their surroundings. He exhaustively studied big universities and small colleges in large East Coast cities such as Boston and Philadelphia, and quieter towns, such as Hartford, Connecticut, and Hanover, New Hampshire, documenting degrees of openness and isolation between "town and gown." Rawn firmly believes that cities and towns enrich the campuses they host, just as the universities play a strong role in the economic, social, and cultural life of their cities. So he studied big and small gestures that make his case: the borders defining a campus, the connections between city streets and campus paths, the open or closed attitudes of buildings.

Rawn's design approach is not entirely empirical, though; his research is always a means to a humanistic end, a sensitivity that extends to both the users of a building and the inhabitants of a city. At the University of Virginia, a campus sadly detached from the ailing heart of downtown Charlottesville, Rawn proposed an urban strategy whereby the university reaches out into the disadvantaged downtown, giving the campus a civic presence it never had and allowing it to jump start the city's economy. While designing a new residence hall for Northeastern University's profoundly urban campus in Boston, Rawn listened carefully to the people who would ultimately inhabit his work. As he did while planning a music building at Philips Exeter Academy in New Hampshire—where he asked students and faculty how they felt about the relationships between practice rooms and public spaces—Rawn interviewed Northeastern students and faculty in order to elicit their opinions about individual buildings. Rawn utilized what his firm calls an "Intensive Design Process," which included a series of two- to three-day mini-charettes with the eventual users of each building. The firm has turned to these kinds of fact-finding missions in many projects, including Seiji Ozawa Hall at Tanglewood, the University of Virginia, and a fire station for Columbus, Indiana.

Such diligent interviewing helps his buildings respond to their users—the final arbiters of his architecture—as well as to the city. As a result of his urbanistic research and interviews with people while designing the dorm at Northeastern, Rawn decided to place public spaces along the ground floor and gave these rooms floor-to-ceiling windows, showing people outside what is taking place inside. He established grand portals that link the campus and city and rendered a large exterior wall less intimidating by inflecting it with a gentle curve. These gestures—at the human scale and the urban scale—perfectly illustrate Rawn's attention to both the comfort of people and the well-being of the city.

William Rawn is no longer a practicing attorney, but it is hard to characterize his new role as an architect. He is not purely an academic, nor a large-scale commercial practitioner, nor a boutique designer. He is an intelligent architect with tremendous sensitivity to the city and the people who live, work, and play in it. Rawn is a great champion of cities. He believes they are thriving centers of human activity, living organisms with complexity and drama, and hubs of rich culture, economy, and society. Rawn's architectural career may have started in the law books, but in the end it is his acute sensitivity to people that makes his case as a truly successful architect.

A Room for

Music

A Room for Music
by William Rawn

A version of the following interview originally appeared in *Seiji Ozawa Hall: A Room for Music*, published by the Boston Symphony Orchestra, Inc., Boston, 1994.

What mission were you given in designing Seiji Ozawa Hall? The ultimate goal was to build a serious concert hall that opened to the outdoors—a daunting assignment. The fundamental question became how to build a structure with thick walls, as you must for optimal acoustics, while, at the same time, opening the building to the landscape. To put it more broadly, the question was how to retain Tanglewood's intimacy and informality, while responding to the intensity of the music.

We faced the inevitable choice—whether to begin from inside the building and con-

sider the acoustical imperatives, as if the hall could be built anyplace, or to begin from the outside, with the setting. In our initial interview with the client, the Boston Symphony Orchestra, we focused on the question of the landscape. We wanted to define the experience and the particular joy of Tanglewood. Later, when we began the design process, we immediately confronted the critical acoustical issues.

What did you say about the landscape in that first interview? What's interesting about Tanglewood, we said, is that, in relation to the main manor house which encloses Stockbridge Bowl, all the music buildings that Eliel and Eero Saarinen designed were put in the background, against the trees, almost like outbuildings. It seemed to me that, even though it's very important, Ozawa Hall should be a background building in keeping with the existing scheme. I think that stance is wonderful; it's one of those things that tells the visitor that Tanglewood has

a very democratic spirit.

How is Tanglewood democratic? Because of the way it's laid out, you feel that everyone is welcome on this grand estate. On weekdays, there is no admission charge. You can casually walk in and listen to very famous musicians teaching their classes. It's the polar opposite of a theme park.

We had to design a concert hall that would seat 1,200 people and create good sight lines for another 2,000 people on the lawn outside. One way to do that is to site the hall like an amphitheater, at the bottom of a steep slope. But the Tanglewood tradition is about spreading your blanket, laying out the picnic, arranging your wine glasses in front of you. It was important for us to preserve that gentle slope—steep enough to allow you to see over the heads of people in front of you, but flat enough to prevent your wine bottle from falling over. That's why we strongly advocated putting the hall higher up the hill.

What about the other half of the mission: the acoustics? Soon after we were chosen, we joined the Boston Symphony Orchestra's design committee in selecting Lawrence Kirkegaard as the acoustician. The acoustical requirements for the hall were critical, particularly for the students, who had to be able to hear themselves and their colleagues as clearly and vividly as possible.

I spent three weeks in Europe looking at major concert halls in Vienna, Berlin, Basel, Zürich, Utrecht, Aldeburgh, and Amsterdam. I visited them in order to understand the spatial qualities and human experience in those halls. Kirkegaard, of course, knows those halls from his own acoustical perspective. He spent a long time with me, explaining the physical reasons why these are great halls. Later, I visited outdoor summer concert venues, including Wolf Trap outside Washington, D.C.; Lake Henrietta in Minneapolis; and Ravinia, near Chicago.

Did any of those halls or outdoor venues stand out as a model for you? Some of the great European concert halls were designed in very simple ways, though they may have been dressed up over time. The Musikverein in Vienna was the one

How does the architecture come together with the acoustics? If you look at the grille, which is basically a grid made up of square openings, you'll see that there's a curve routed into the wood. We did that on Kirkegaard's advice, so as not to allow a rhythmic pattern to develop across the surface. If the surface of the wood were flat and regular, a disconcerting sound pattern might develop. But because the surfaces of the grille are hollowed out in slightly irregular curves, the sound is diffused when it bounces off the railing.

19th-century hall with a very strong architectural presence, as well as great acoustics, so it became an ideal for me. Maltings Hall at Aldeburgh, England, is in a beautiful rural setting like Tanglewood; it also seemed to be a very powerful place.

What did you find most striking about the Musikverein's architecture? I feel that the most important visual element in a concert hall is the railing along the balcony and the loge boxes. Once a hall is filled with people, that railing becomes the most important architectural element, aside from the stage. In Vienna, the railing elements are gilded and highly ornate.

At Tanglewood, we wanted to be less formal, but we also wanted to capture some of that spatial quality. So we developed a grille made out of teakwood for our railing element. The teak is handsome, but it's also modest, weathers well, and reminds people of the outdoors.

Is irregularity the key to the acoustics? Kirkegaard worries about routine patterns, so he wants everything to be slightly off-alignment. Generally, he wants sound to be reflected back from all the surfaces as fully as possible, to give it depth and richness. But if any two elements in the hall are perfectly symmetrical, there is a danger that the sound will start to echo as it bounces back and forth. You want the attributes of symmetry, but not perfect symmetry.

For example, Kirkegaard's ideal side walls would be, maybe, half a degree off parallel. We haven't done that at Tanglewood, but we did find ways to bring the surfaces of the side walls slightly out of alignment. In fact, we've canted elements all over the hall.

Is the ceiling canted, too? Kirkegaard said the ceiling had to be coffered, though not with perfect curves. So we built the ceiling out of precast concrete elements that look like upside-down bathtubs, each 21 feet long. They are not perfect concave circles or ellipses.

Why such a heavy ceiling? It had to be. The walls had to be heavy, too. The building is a brick and concrete block shell; it has very thick side walls, which keep the bass notes in the hall. Bass notes will go right through a thin wood wall, and only the treble will reflect back. That's why the great halls of the world have very thick side walls, which are generally parallel.

If the hall has to be so heavy and enclosed, how can it also be open to the landscape?

seating is made out of plastic. That seemed inappropriate for Tanglewood; at the same time, we knew the seats would have to stand up to hard use because of the climate. So we chose teak, which is very durable.

Is there a visual connection among these elements, apart from being made of wood? The backrests of the seats pick up the grid motif of the balcony railing, as do the wooden grid elements fitted between the coffers of the ceiling. The grille is picked up on the exterior balconies, too. That's another way of weaving the wood throughout the building, through this repetition of grid patterns.

Essentially, Ozawa Hall is a brick shell into which we've woven a wooden frame. The brick is what holds in the sound; the wood holds the audience. Inside, the balconies and loge boxes are wood. Outside, the foyer, platforms, and arcades are all made of wood. Structurally, the foyers and balconies open up the building and give it a human scale; in terms of material, they help the building blend in with the surrounding landscape.

The timber that's exposed to the weather is Alaskan yellow cedar, which turns gray as it weathers, like the shingles of Cape Cod cottages. The timber under the roof of the arcade is Douglas fir. All of the big, heavy timbers have been salvaged from old piers and train trestles. They don't look like they've been used before, but they've already dried out and won't shrink any further.

We designed chairs made of plantation teak. For outdoor venues, commercially available

Each time, of course, we try to make the grid a little different, so it's not relentless.

How have you handled the hall's windows? We couldn't allow ourselves very many windows, because bass notes go through glass as easily as they go through wood. So we've built glass-block clerestory windows high up; they pick up the square grid motif again. At the northeast end of the hall, behind the stage, we have tall, narrow windows, the shape of which is echoed by the vertical backrests of the chairs.

The vertical windows let you see as much of the outside as possible, without putting in too much glass. They may remind you of organ pipes at the rear of the stage in many great concert halls—but that was probably an after-the-fact rationalization for us. We would have loved to have made the whole back wall out of glass, but that just wouldn't work acoustically.

Do you feel you've captured a sense of the outdoors in the hall? You'll certainly get light through the clerestory windows and, from the second balcony, you'll see the trees. As the concert begins, the windows behind the stage will let you see the sky change from sunset to twilight to night. It was important that each of the side doors had glass, so you'd get glimpses of the outside from the seats. Of course, during major concerts, the big door to the lawn—what we call the barn door—will be open to the audience outside. When that door is open, the feeling of the lawn definitely comes into the hall.

be at least that tall—taller, in fact, because we needed an attic space for ventilation and lighting. The curved roof allows us to modify the effect of that height. We're able to go from a 66-foot-high ridgeline to a 42-foot-high cornice line, while keeping the interior at 50 feet.

How else have you tried to maintain a human scale? During the early phases of design, we talked a lot about a community coming together for music. That's why we dispensed with the proscenium, so you wouldn't have the performers on one side of a divide and the audience on the other. Most European halls, including the Musikverein in Vienna

The barn door should be seen as a side door opening to the garden, but we did not deliberately intend for the building to be read as a barn. Obviously, the curved barrel roof is one of the hall's distinctive features. When we were designing the building, we found a 19th-century Shaker school in Mt. Lebanon, New York, with that roof form. That's the only building of this shape that we found near Tanglewood.

Why did you want a curved roof? It presents a very soft edge to the sky. A pitched roof with a gable end presents a strong ridge against the sky, as does the edge of a flat roof. We didn't want anything that hard-edged, because Tanglewood is essentially a soft, comfortable landscape.

We were also trying to figure out ways to bring the scale of the building down to a human proportion. Kirkegaard told us that the ceiling in the hall had to be 50 feet high, otherwise we wouldn't get the proper acoustic volume. The building had to

and the Concertgebouw in Amsterdam, lack a proscenium stage, so there is precedent for such a move. By creating balconies and loge boxes, we designed Ozawa Hall so you'd see the faces of the people all around you, in the side balconies and in the seats behind the stage.

It sounds like a Friends meeting house. I wouldn't claim any direct influence like that, but we did want to give people the sense of being together in a room, which we simply called "a room for music."

Our consultants at Theatre Projects in Connecticut and London gave us wonderful ideas about how to make the space very intimate by making the balconies as tight and low as possible and by making the building as snug as we could. We saved every inch possible.

What about the support structure, the Leonard Bernstein Performers Pavilion? We designed the Performers Pavilion so it could be built as simply and frugally as possible, using wood-frame con-

16

The plantation teak chairs, designed by William Rawn Associates, continue the pattern of wood throughout the space and lend a warmth to the hall.

struction. It's a simple one-story structure, with an open courtyard in the middle. It provides changing rooms, a green room, recording equipment, a small library, and piano storage.

Perhaps its best feature is the open courtyard—something you'd never build in New England. But since we didn't have to heat this building during the winter, we could have a courtyard, which can be an informal green room for the performers, a gathering place after concerts, or a hang-out spot for students.

What's your response to objec-

did it enter into grand concert halls. So we've come full circle with history here.

It's been important to think of the magic of Tanglewood and to balance the spirit of the landscape and its informality with a commitment to the intensity of the musical experience. That's why we tried to fight against formality in Ozawa Hall by bringing people close to one another, by putting in as many windows as we could, by using the teak grilles to provide a warmer feeling. This building is trying to find a balance between the seriousness of a concert hall and the informality that's such an essential element of Tanglewood.

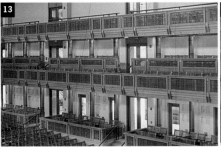

tions that you designed a brick building for Tanglewood? Nothing else at Tanglewood is built out of brick, but we recognized that there's a very eclectic mix of building materials and building styles. That gave us tremendous design freedom. More importantly, Massachusetts' building code requires that any public assembly building over 35 feet high must be made of fire-resistant material, which means it cannot be built from wood. The only exception is for churches. That's the law, and we can't do a thing about it. We could have designed a metal structure, or maybe something in poured concrete; but it seemed that those materials would violate the landscape.

Now, at the end of the process, how do you regard the building? When I began this project, I started reading about the history of concert halls, and learned that in 17th-century Europe, concerts often took place in the garden. Music came indoors in the 18th century; only in the 19th century

(1) The Tanglewood tradition of picnicking on the lawn is preserved in Seiji Ozawa Hall. While working on designs for Seiji Ozawa Hall, William Rawn traveled around Europe visiting major concert halls. Pictured here are the Musikvereinssaal in Vienna (2), the Stadt-Casino in Basel (3), seating in the Philharmonie Hall in Berlin (4), the Konzerthaus (formerly Schauspielhaus) in Berlin (5), and the stage of Berlin's Philharmonic Hall (6). At Seiji Ozawa Hall, the use of open wood grilles carries through many aspects of the design, from the grid of the balcony and arcade rails (7) to soffits at the balcony ceilings (8) to the vertical grilles of the sound absorption panels (9). The open wood grilles lend an intimate and informal character to the interior balconies and exterior arcades (10, 11).

(12) Seiji Ozawa Hall's curved roof presents a soft line against the sky while allowing the building to accommodate the hall's required 50-foot acoustical volume.
(13) The use of wood on interior balconies, loge boxes, and seats creates a feeling of intimacy and warmth.
(14) The architect designed Ozawa Hall's plantation teak chairs.
(15) A horizontal brick pattern marks the base of the arcade walls.

Through large windows behind the stage, audience members can watch the sky fade to black as night concerts begin (facing page).

Summer concerts at Tanglewood
are celebrated from the lawn of
Seiji Ozawa Hall.

Seiji Ozawa Hall at Tanglewood
Boston Symphony Orchestra, Lenox, Massachusetts 1994

Seiji Ozawa Hall meets the challenge of creating a space that is both open and closed— open to the views and spirit of the revered Berkshire landscape, yet enclosed to meet the requirements for world-class acoustics.

The 1,180-seat concert hall at Tanglewood, the summertime home for the Boston Symphony Orchestra, has a form based on the rectangular "shoebox" proportions—in this case, roughly a double cube in volume—of the world's greatest and most acoustically desirable concert halls, including the Musikvereinssaal in Vienna, the Concertgebouw in Amsterdam, and Boston's Symphony Hall. The interior, conceived by the architect as a "room for music," invokes the intimate and democratic community found in historic New England meeting houses. The music hall's clerestory windows, glass doors, and tall, narrow windows establish a strong connection to the outdoors by providing natural light, breezes, and views of the surrounding landscape. In his book *Concert and Opera Halls: How They Sound*, author Leo Beranek recounts *New York Times* music critic Edward Rothstein's description of Ozawa Hall: "[It] is precisely what a concert hall should be: a resonant, warm space that comes to life with sound."

Seiji Ozawa Hall serves the Tanglewood Music Center, a summer fellowship program for young professionals founded in the late 1930s. Named after the Boston Symphony's longtime director, the $9.7 million hall provides a venue for the major vocal and instrumental performances, student recitals, and commercial recordings that were previously staged in the existing 1941 opera theater, a barn-like auditorium designed by Eliel and Eero Saarienen.

The massing of the "shoebox" allows the six-story volume (necessary for proper acoustics) to fit into the lower scale of buildings in the Berkshires. A large exterior vault made of lead-coated copper crowns the simple, shed-like brick volume. The curved roof and side arcades break down the size of the building to fit the scale of other structures at Tanglewood. On the hall's long flanks, post-and-beam timber porches above the open arcades shelter exterior staircases, which lead to balconies inside the hall. Adjacent to the concert hall, the Leonard Bernstein building, which is organized around a private exterior courtyard, serves as an informal gathering place for the musicians and contains the backstage areas of the concert hall.

The interior of Ozawa Hall is an intimate setting without a proscenium separating the audience and performer; instead, audience members face each other as well as the musicians. Two levels of seating balconies, bound by gridded teak screens that double as important acoustic reflectors, wrap the sides and the front of the hall. Filled with warm woods, such as teak and Douglas fir, the airy hall is engineered to withstand temperature and humidity fluctuations inside the non-winterized structure. The interior is also lined with slatted wood seats designed by the architect.

At the rear of the hall, a series of large teak-clad barn doors slide open to reveal a 50-foot-wide aperture that exposes the hall to a gently sloping lawn, which serves as additional seating for 2,000 listeners. Ambient and direct amplification replicate the sound from within the hall for the outdoor audience. The doors can be shut to seal the hall when musicians are recording.

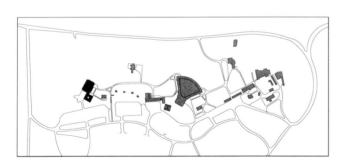

Site Plan

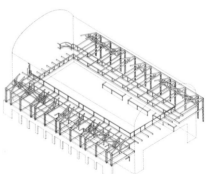

Diagram: Interpenetrating Timber Plane

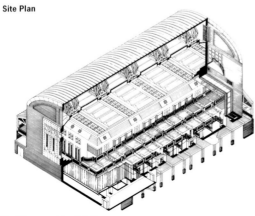

Dual Axonometric of Hall

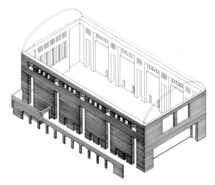

Diagram: Acoustic Shell/Masonry Box

The form of the hall mirrors the rolling hills of the Berkshires in Western Massachusetts (facing page). At night, the glow of the hall reveals a constant communication between the building and the landscape (above).

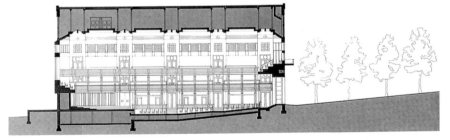

Longitudinal Section

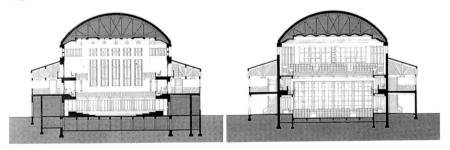

Transverse Section Looking East   **Transverse Section Looking West**

The large barn door opens the
concert hall to the lawn, providing
direct views of the stage from
the outside.

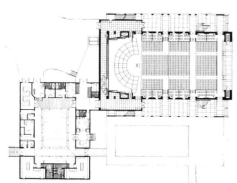

Main Level Floor Plan

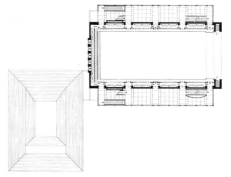

First Balcony Floor Plan

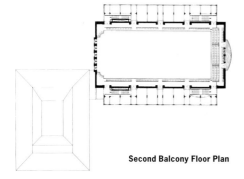

Second Balcony Floor Plan

Ozawa Hall creates a sense of warmth with its wood balconies, wood seats, and wood floor (above). When filled, the hall establishes a sense of intimacy where the audience members, facing each other, surround the musicians (facing page).

Continuous wood balconies on the interior (this page) and arcades on the exterior (facing page) provide a warm and hand-crafted counterpoint to the solid acoustic enclosure of the hall.

Like Louis Kahn's library across the street, the music building celebrates the student on its exterior façade.

Exeter Music Building
Phillips Exeter Academy, Exeter, New Hampshire 1995

The Exeter Music Building uses a modern building form to help define a major open space at the heart of a traditional campus.

This new music building at Phillips Exeter Academy, a prestigious preparatory school, fills in the "missing tooth" of the main quadrangle, a space otherwise marked by Georgian brick buildings and by Louis Kahn's iconic 1967–72 library, which is located across the street. The new building subsumes a small, gutted 1959 music facility. It holds a large orchestral rehearsal hall and recital hall, a choral rehearsal space, music classrooms, teaching studios, practice rooms, and a music laboratory.

The 22,500-square-foot, $2.8 million facility celebrates the idea of ensemble in music—whether an ensemble of two, four, or 80 students. The main entry façade responds to the ensemble activities of the music students with large windows that reveal the major rehearsal and common spaces. This straightforward brick façade acknowledges—and distinguishes itself from—the Kahn building, which, by contrast, celebrates the individual student at his or her carrel.

A pair of interior "courts," which are informal, double-height spaces, provide communal gathering areas and surround all the rehearsal spaces, teaching studios, and practice rooms. This arrangement solves a problem endemic to most complex music buildings: the "rabbit warren" of tiny practice rooms stretched along narrow winding corridors.

The building's rectilinear face respects the formal nature of the existing quadrangle. Its brick cladding, cast-stone trim, and lead-coated copper vaulted roof relate to the scale and character of the older campus buildings. The simple interior palette is warmed by cherry wood trim, doors, and lockers, as well as abundant natural light.

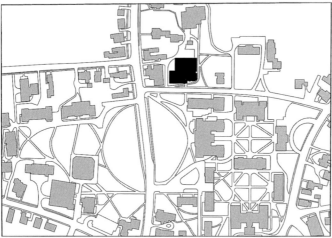

The Music Building creates a strong edge and corner to the Main Quad (above). An interior "entry court" serves as the main gathering space, ideal for impromptu rehearsals or performances (facing page).

Site Plan

Section

Isometric

Second Floor Plan

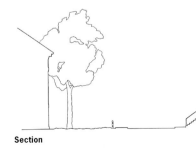

Section

The small, nearly cubic chapel comprises two faces of glass window walls and two faces of Deer Isle granite.

Glavin Family Chapel
Babson College, Wellesley, Massachusetts 1997

The Glavin Family Chapel uses a simple, abstract form to create a strong and contemplative space that engages its natural surroundings while accommodating the requirements of a multi-denominational congregation.

41

This small $3.4 million chapel, sited on the slope of a hill overlooking the Babson College campus, provides a worship space for 150 people. Two walls of solid Deer Isle granite and two walls of solid glass form the nearly cubic (44 feet x 44 feet x 40 feet), 5,100-square-foot building. The solid walls are cherry wood on the interior. The glass walls, which face a densely wooded site, combine clear glass and stained glass panels designed by artist Peter McGrain.

Although the chapel is located at a major campus crossroads, the architects designed a tranquil retreat from the buzz of the campus. A curved stair leads visitors to the entrance wing, which is wrapped in glass and inset with sheets of rice paper that diffuse light and screen views of the surrounding landscape. Paneled ebony and cherry doors with silver inlays, designed by artist Rick Wrigley, open into an airy, 30-foot-high sanctuary crowned by a curved wooden ceiling, a boat hull shape that counterpoints the chapel's strong rectilinear shell. The cedar planks of the hull-shaped ceiling, crafted by Mitch Ryerson, combine with cherry wall paneling and floors to create a warm atmosphere inside the chapel. The mood of the space is peaceful, contemplative, and tranquil. The designers established abstract iconography for the chapel, since it serves worshippers of a number of faiths.

The square plan permits a range of orthogonal, diagonal, and circular seating arrangements; the solid or glass walls can form the backdrop to any service. The glass walls face clusters of deciduous trees, which offer protection from the heat in the summer and create dappled light in the winter. The chapel joins two other new buildings designed by William Rawn Associates at Babson College: the campus center and campus theater.

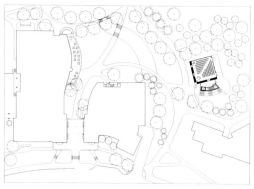

Site Plan

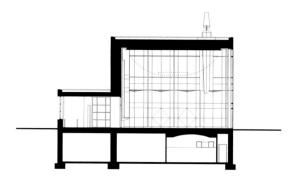

Section

Seating Options

Beneath the hull-shaped wooden
ceiling, the flexible space allows
for a wide variety of seating
arrangements facing either the
windows (above) or the cherry-
paneled interior (facing page).

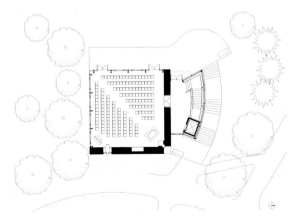

Main Floor Plan

Lower Level Floor Plan

A crescent-shaped dining facility, constructed of glass, steel, and wood, embraces the rear edge of the amphitheater, opposite the stage, shown here as a model (facing page, top), and in full use (facing page, bottom).

The Pavilion at Symphony Lake
Cary, North Carolina 2001

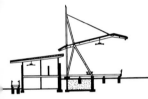

Section—Center Wing

Partial Elevation of Crescent

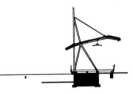

Section—Outer Wing

The Pavilion at Symphony Lake employs high technology glass and steel to achieve a sense of transparency and luminosity that accentuates its wooded lakeside setting.

The $12.5 million covered pavilion and open amphitheater in Cary, North Carolina, will be the cultural center for this fast-growing city just outside Raleigh and will serve as one of the summer homes of the North Carolina Symphony. The amphitheater—conceived as a clearing in the tall pinewoods—provides outdoor lawn seating for 7,000 people with views of the performance pavilion and Symphony Lake beyond. In addition, a crescent-shaped dining facility, constructed of glass, steel, and wood, is located behind the lawn. This structure creates a formal edge that provides a sense of enclosure while focusing on the pavilion and the lake.

Eighty-foot poles, inspired by the tall thin pine trees of the Piedmont area, support a suspended glass canopy that floats over the performers and shelters the stage. Composed of more than 100 laminated glass panels, the large, translucent canopy glows at night like an enormous lantern. In addition, the canopy contains hidden speakers, lighting, and acoustical equipment. Glass walls surrounding the stage allow the pine trees and the lake to define its perimeter.

The highly flexible amphitheater can support a variety of performances, including symphony, dance, theater, and opera. The exposed stage rigging, for example, supports drapes that transform the concert shell into a full proscenium theater, while the choral loft turns into an orchestral loft for dance and opera performances. The covered crescent-shaped building can hold 500 for a seated dinner or 700 for a lecture.

The theater's acoustics are a combination of natural and electronic sound amplification. A computer-enhanced audio system and a grid of speakers hidden among the trees boost natural sound and generate the warmth of interior reverberation in an outdoor setting. The patterned glass shell behind the stage directs sound toward the audience.

48

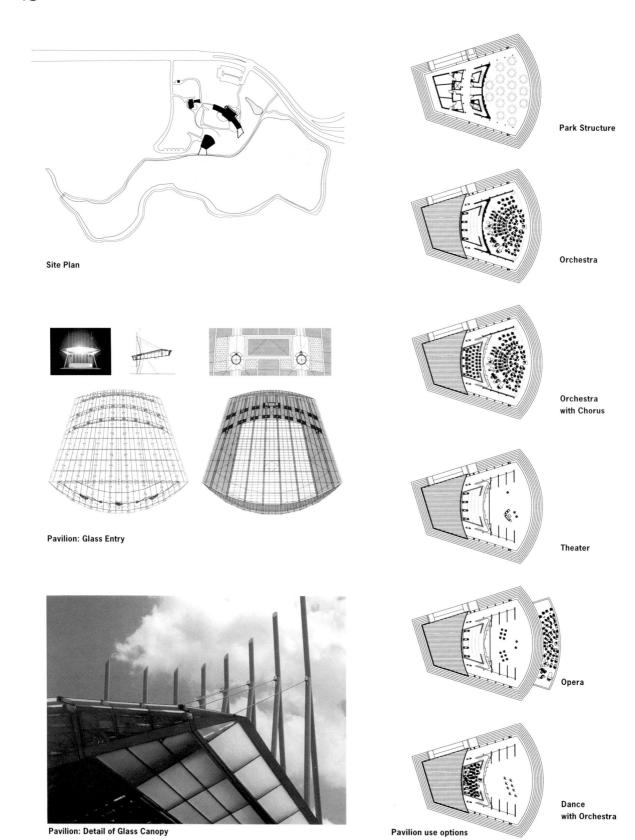

Site Plan

Pavilion: Glass Entry

Pavilion: Detail of Glass Canopy

Park Structure

Orchestra

Orchestra
with Chorus

Theater

Opera

Dance
with Orchestra

Pavilion use options

With a lawn that seats 7,000 audience members, Symphony Lake's amphitheater can support a wide variety of performance types, including dance, theater, symphony, and opera (top). The glass canopy sheltering the stage comprises over 100 laminated glass panels (bottom).

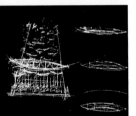   

This large concert hall will serve as the year-round home for the Santa Rosa Symphony, as well as a summer venue for major orchestras.

Donald and Maureen Green Music Center

Sonoma State University, Sonoma County, California
2003

With its disciplined orchestration of distinct architectural forms, defined exterior spaces, and permeable or transparent building surfaces, the Green Music Center roots the new concert hall, recital hall, and music facilities into a truly unique Sonoma County environment.

Located at the edge of the Sonoma State University campus, the Green Music Center will double as the year-round home of the Santa Rosa Symphony and other regional music groups, and will serve as a summer venue for major orchestras. A set of large glass windows facing the archetypal Sonoma Hills to the east will mark the 1,400-seat concert hall, a space with loge boxes and two surrounding balconies. Large doors at the rear of the hall will open the space onto a lawn, where an audience of up to 10,000 people—many with views of the stage—can listen to musical performances surrounded by views of the hills of Sonoma County.

The design acknowledges the architectural traditions of Sonoma County with an entry courtyard that organizes access to the two halls and to the large lawns beyond. The strong linear wall, which forms the entry edge, organizes the separate building elements. The arc-like curve of the roof is an iconic gesture. A system of timber beams, covered walkways, and an entry elevation of wood slats alternated with glass inserts emphasize the permeability of the entire complex.

A smaller, flexible recital hall, containing 300 seats and a concert organ, focuses on the demands of serious choral recitals for groups of up to 150 performers, as well as smaller chamber music ensembles. Like the main concert hall, the recital hall will celebrate intimacy between audience and performer in a space with high ceilings and windows that open to direct views of the hills. The project's educational component will include academic offices, rehearsal rooms, and a music library.

Construction will begin in the summer of 2002.

The gently curving roof shapes the
Strathmore Concert Hall's tall
acoustic volume while reflecting the
hills in the background.

Strathmore
Concert Hall
Montgomery
County, Maryland
2004

The use of curved forms and canted glass panels brings an urbanity to a carefully sited cultural building, while tying it to a powerfully lyrical landscape.

The architects designed Strathmore Concert Hall and Educational Facility, located in North Bethesda, just outside Washington, D.C., as the cultural center of Montgomery County, Maryland. Serving as the second home of the Baltimore Symphony Orchestra, the building balances the complex, quasi-urban life of the Rockville Pike Corridor with the scenic qualities of rolling lawns and gardens. The short walk from the local Metro stop—a glass-enclosed subway station and adjacent parking structure— winds through groves of trees and gardens, engaging patrons with the natural beauty of the site.

An iconic form, consisting of a curved roof and stone cladding, celebrates the music facility's setting and purpose. The curved roof satisfies acoustical needs in the concert hall, while also symbolizing the fluid nature of music and reflecting the profiles of the hills in the distance. Stone cladding dignifies the primary music room volumes while the back-of-house components are clad in modest concrete panels. A 60-foot-high glass lobby overlooks the landscape in a dramatic way, and a 200-foot-long glass promenade connects the lobby to the entry.

The 2,000-seat Concert Hall supports the needs of a major symphony orchestra as well as local orchestras and popular artists. Curved interior walls, which create a comfortable and embracing relationship between audience and performer, are perforated for acoustic transparency to the "shoebox" enclosure beyond. Grillage finishes, paneling, and wood and stainless steel trim give the hall a warm, contemporary elegance. Acoustic variability accommodates a wide range of programming possibilities, including orchestral music, chamber music, choral recitals, world music, dance, popular performances, and lectures. The Educational Facility will provide classes for the children in the Montgomery County School System, among other students.

Curved walls and balconies create a sense of intimacy between musicians and audience within the 2,000-seat hall.

Where the the Water

City Meets

Where the City Meets the Water
by William Rawn

Based on lectures at the Museum of Fine Arts, Boston, March 18, 1992, and the Parks Council and Municipal Art Society, New York, October 29, 1990

City-making is an art form. Likewise, it is the result of the interplay between design and politics. Look at the great waterfront cities of the world. They reflect the balance of civic, cultural, and economic forces that has led to great design. In cities such as Paris, Barcelona, and San Francisco—or small towns like Edgartown, Massachusetts, and Stonington, Connecticut—public policy and design culture have joined in a successful collaboration.

However, in late 20th-century America, city-making has lost its balance: witness cities like Los Angeles, Phoenix, Atlanta, or the newer

of the water—the very water that fostered the founding of Boston in the first place.

Where the city meets the water immediately conjures romantic, indeed poetic, images—the opening lines of *Moby Dick*, the Mississippi riverfronts of Mark Twain, or the fishing shacks in the contemporary poetry of Erica Funkhauser. For architects, where the city meets the water raises boundless formal opportunities and creates fundamental responsibilities. It is about that ultimate boundary between man and nature, that fixed line where human beings must come to a stop.

so-called "edge cities," such as Tyson's Corner, near Washington, D.C. In a time of recurring interest in urban quality of life, many older cities with strong waterfronts find themselves with a major advantage over the randomly expanding cities and suburbs of the 20th century. And, almost inevitably, those older cities have the potential for a strong waterfront, as they were originally founded because of their waterfront locations—on a harbor, a river, or a canal.

Boston is a powerful example of a waterfront city. From its unplanned Beacon Hill to its highly planned Back Bay, from its natural harbor edge to its manmade beaches, evidence of a commitment to city-making abounds. More recently, with the encouragement of activist citizens, architects, and public officials, the waterfront has emerged as Boston's great 21st-century planning and architectural opportunity. There is an extraordinary chance to bring city-making back to the edge

Where the city meets the water: Is it where the ordered, patterned, rectilinear city meets the natural, organic, meandering water's edge? Or is it where the enigmatic, irrational, and unpredictable city meets the continuous, linear, fixed edge of the water? Obviously, it is both; these ambiguities are what excite me as an architect.

From the opening paragraphs of *Moby Dick*:

There now is your insular city of the Manhattoes, belted round by wharves as Indian isles by coral reefs...Right and left, the streets take you waterward...What do you see?—Posted like silent sentinels all around the town, stand thousands upon thousands of mortal men fixed in ocean reveries...Here come more crowds, pacing straight for the water, and seemingly bound for a dive. Nothing will content them but the extremest limit of the land...Inlanders all, they come from lanes and alleys, streets and avenues—north, east, south, and west. Yet here they all unite.

If cities are to recapture their waterfronts, those waterfronts must reflect the urbanity of cities. It's folly to separate cities from water, whether by a wall of high buildings, by fences and private enclaves, or by open spaces that are windswept and unsafe. To connect the city to its waterfront we must do four things: 1) Celebrate the continuous and public edge of the water, creating continuous—or nearly con-

Commonwealth Avenue in Boston's Back Bay, on a tree-lined street of three-deckers in Dorchester, and on a lane of clapboard houses in a small town on the Cape. It is particularly true in the commercial center of any town or city. The continuous street edge becomes a fundamental first tenet of city-building, regardless of historic period. It can be a group of buildings from different eras in Stockbridge, Massachusetts, or a row of 20th-century apartment houses in Miami Beach.

The second rule of thumb in the making of cities would be to observe that the most

tinuous—paths along the water. 2) Make certain that areas near the water are vibrant and urbane. These qualities are best achieved when an important street, perhaps a Main Street, is near the harbor's edge. 3) Establish connector streets and views connecting the water with the important streets where people spend most of their time. 4) Make certain that the building patterns of the city are permitted to extend to the water's edge (remembering that a building parallel to the water blocks views while a building perpendicular to the water allows broader views from behind).

When we talk about waterfronts as integral parts of the city, we need to address that element that is most integral to the city: the nature of the urban street—its continuous edges and its two-sided character. Even with buildings of differing roof heights, successful streets tend to have a continuous edge whereby all the buildings line up on the street and become part of a greater whole. This is true on

successful urban streets are two-sided. On a major street in New York City or a small street in an Italian hill town, retail activity is found almost always on two-sided streets. There is something in the human spirit that likes this character, this sense that you can see or feel the range of choices when you walk down a two-sided retail street. Of the major commercial streets in any culture, 99.9 percent of them are two-sided. Waterfront settings need these kinds of spaces in order to integrate into the life of the city. Main Street in most American cities fits this model. Rodeo Drive in Beverly Hills, the street with the highest cost per square foot of retail space in the Los Angeles basin, is a two-sided street. Newbury Street is an excellent Boston example. A two-sided street connects the Gulf of Mexico to the Atlantic Ocean in Key West, Florida. Ben Thompson brilliantly applied this two-sided concept in several parts of Boston's Quincy Market. Even a county road, in New England or Provençe, feels special when lined by trees on two sides.

Take a look at the main streets of two vibrant Massachusetts seacoast towns, Edgartown and Nantucket; they are perpendicular to the waterfront. These streets promote city-building. The entire town congregates on the main street and walks down to the wharf on the harbor, a very public place that is central to the spirit of the town. Other seacoast models place the main street parallel to the water. In Woods Hole and Provincetown, Massachusetts, or in Stonington, Connecticut, the main street looks

demands a different treatment. Harbors, by definition, are well protected; rarely are they subject to flooding. The only movement in a harbor is the tide going up and down, so buildings can come close to the water's edge; human beings can safely get right up to the water's edge.

Buildings should be as responsive to the waterfront as the rest of the city. In Boston, Rowes Wharf, designed by Skidmore, Owings & Merrill with the strong help of the Boston Redevelopment Authority's design guidelines, touches the edge of the water. Its human scale is wonderful. Public access is

between buildings to see the harbor. This street reflects a town that is a year-round destination, one that is not windswept and inhumane in the winter. For instance, Provincetown has long, linear buildings lined up along the main street that connects to the water. At intervals along that main street, cross streets intersect and extend with public town landings to the water's edge. Everybody is constantly aware of the water, and everybody has access to the water. In addition, walking down the main street, one constantly catches glimpses of the water between the buildings. One is protected from the wind; one experiences the water and has access to its edge.

The key to forging a precise relationship between the city and the water is to understand the nature of the water. Boston, for instance, is special because of its harbor, which has qualities very different from those of a river edge, an ocean edge, or a canal edge. Each type of waterfront

provided along the edge. Importantly, the pedestrian walkway that runs behind the Rowes Wharf finger piers provides an active urban path parallel to the harbor, ensuring another active connection to the city.

Our firm designed affordable housing at the water's edge in the Charlestown Navy Yard. There we responded specifically to the Navy Yard's linear buildings and First Avenue, its main street. We felt that it was important to integrate our building into the fabric of the Navy Yard. The housing is about significant gable-ended buildings, long linear buildings, and special buildings on the water's edge. Here, the city is about strong, rectilinear, very predictable forms. Our building fits into that pattern of the city, while celebrating its intersection with the meandering edge of the harbor.

Rivers are constantly changing and constantly moving as they build new channels and create new sandbars. They are also prone to flooding, particularly on this continent; historically, river cities have carefully organized themselves to respond to the unpredictable and sometimes dangerous edge of the river.

Unlike most American cities, which are located on one side of a river—for instance, St. Louis or Louisville—Rochester, New York, straddles its river, the Genesee. In our urban design work there, we were inspired by European cities that similarly straddle their rivers, cities like Paris or Florence. Rochester's river is glorious; it includes industrial flood control elements as well as an 80-foot waterfall

Copacabana or Ipanema beaches. Miami Beach is analogous: a beachfront tourist town evolving into a thriving beachfront city.

Compare these with the more common American model, for example, Rohobeth Beach, Delaware. Very popular in July and August, it is cold, windswept, and relatively deserted during the rest of the year. If one wants to create a real city along the ocean's edge, one must design it to thrive year round. The open, single-sided boardwalk is not enough.

Our firm has worked with the town of Hull, Massachusetts, another resort "boardwalk"

in the middle of the city. Our study led to zoning recommendations for the first block-and-a-half back from the water on each shore. These recommendations, integrated into the city's zoning code, emphasized not only the creation of a continuous edge along the river, but also the strengthening of the connection between the river and the important streets a block away.

Oceanfront cities are more rare. These cities have a different economic raison d'etre. Not usually founded on historic models of commerce, their location is typically based on recreation and leisure. Given the predictability of tidal movements, like harbors, they are safe places for urban settlement.

Probably the world's greatest oceanfront city is Rio de Janeiro, where the major parts of the city literally open up directly to the beach; imagine if Lexington Avenue in New York City opened to the beach. That is the level of urbanity of

town. Hull has a strong city grid that continues to the water's edge. In the late 19th century, amusement parks and grand waterfront hotels were built along what Thoreau called one of the most beautiful beaches in the world. Today parking lots and sad penny arcades mark that same area—not sufficient even for the center of a small town. We developed a plan for Hull by recommending the creation of a redesigned town center, one based on a two-sided main street. It was predicated on the importance of maintaining the view to the beach from the main street. Buildings could be carefully designed along the street edge to permit the views of the water that everyone in Hull wanted to preserve, yet these buildings could provide the requisite sense of enclosure to the main street to establish a true urbanity.

A fourth city type is the canal city. Amsterdam is the great example. Venice is obviously another. These cities are totally man-made,

66

The new Pavilion at Symphony Lake, shown here at a Fourth of July celebration, provides the town of Cary with a cultural center overlooking the water.

well-protected, and carefully controlled. Yet they are very beautiful. Amsterdam is organized with a series of radial streets emanating from the city center. Invariably these are two-sided commercial streets. Perpendicular to those are one-sided residential and warehouse streets along the circumferential canals. With landscape architects Brown and Rowe, our firm designed Boarding House Park for the National Park Service in Lowell, Massachusetts. Lowell is a city dominated by wonderful man-made canals; its buildings often touch the water's edge. Yet, much of the city is now dominated by parking lots.

environment, and with open space. It also reflects a powerful quality-of-life comparative advantage for a city vis-a-vis its suburbs.

Cities are under stress in this country. Take the examples of great 19th-century cities like St. Louis and Cleveland, which were founded on major rivers for transportation or other economic advantages. They have the special qualities of open space, beauty, and ambiance because of their setting, yet these qualities are lost today. Drab suburbs are taking economic power away from downtown. Go to St. Louis and look care-

In our plan for the Boarding House Park, we created a linear pavilion building to strengthen the canal edge of the park. This pavilion was transparent enough to generate views of the canals and the mill buildings beyond, yet opaque enough to form a fourth embracing edge to the park. Established as a music stage, the pavilion was designed to be simultaneously a theater, a marketplace, a trolley stop, and a site for ethnic dance performance. It has become the site of a famous folk festival. In addition, we designed the pavilion as a civic space, celebrating the open space on the canal. Within a year of completion, its civic nature was so obvious that Paul Tsongas, native son of Lowell, chose it as the site to announce his candidacy for president in 1992.

Where the city meets the water, for the public and for public officials, is also a place of immense controversy. The water's edge clearly reflects America's current preoccupation with history, with the

fully; it barely touches its waterfront. That could be changed.

Today, Boston has a powerful opportunity; the amount of activity that could take place on its waterfront in the next 50 years is extraordinary and the choice is becoming simple: Does Boston build a real city along the water's edge or does it build undifferentiated open space, a glorified suburb, at its harbor's edge? One choice references a history and urbanity that is part of city-building; the other once again turns its back on those qualities that are so much a part of the city. This is a choice that many cities face today. A city is a fundamentally democratic place, a mix of rich and poor, young and old, black and white, a place that derives its vibrancy from interaction and diversity. Bring these qualities of the city to the waterfront, to the port city, the place where that exchange and interchange has always taken place. The opportunities are boundless.

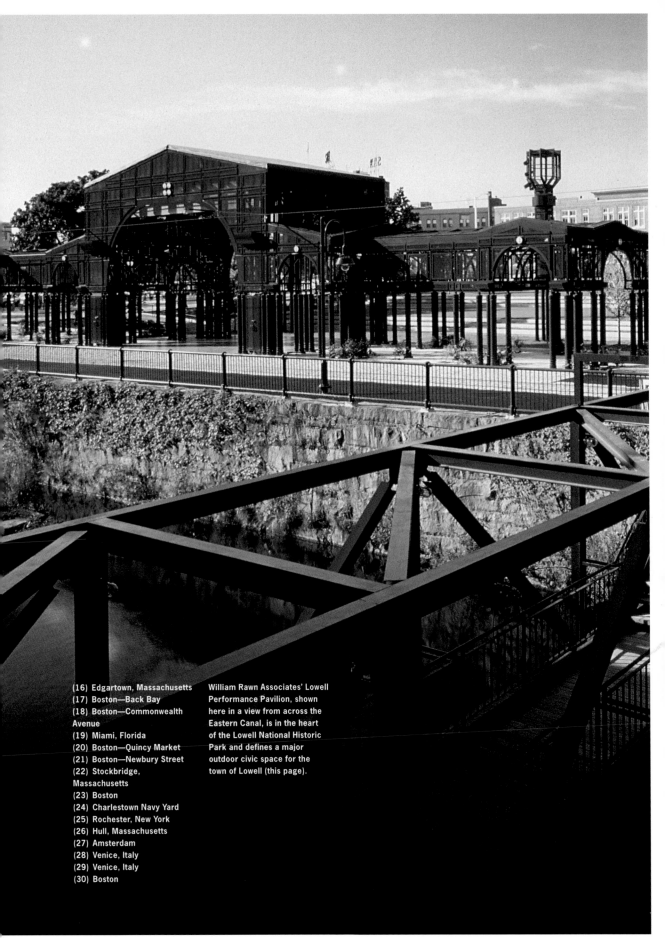

William Rawn Associates' Lowell
Performance Pavilion, shown
here in a view from across the
Eastern Canal, is in the heart
of the Lowell National Historic
Park and defines a major
outdoor civic space for the
town of Lowell (this page).

The Charlestown rowhouses comprise 50 units of affordable housing along Boston Harbor, connecting the street to the water.

Charlestown Navy Yard Rowhouses

Boston, Massachusetts 1988

Strong, simple forms synthesizing a waterfront pattern can elevate affordable housing into a tool for city-building at the water's edge.

The Boston-based Bricklayers and Laborers Non-Profit Housing Corporation sponsored the design and construction of 50 units of affordable housing in the historic former Navy Yard on Boston Harbor. In order to respond to the 19th-century context without simply replicating the existing forms, the architects created a mix of stacked townhouses and two taller structures. The architects designed the 3/4-acre project to strengthen the urban conditions of the site, while celebrating the building's connection to the waterfront.

Recognizing the importance of the Navy Yard's two-sided street, which runs parallel to the water's edge, the complex's northern end strengthens First Avenue as the area's main street with a gabled, seven-story shed structure that reinforces the pattern of long, gable-ended buildings facing First Avenue. An archway through the structure permits views of the water from the avenue, further activating this main street.

Perpendicular to the gabled structure is a long, wharf-inspired, three-story bar that extends to the harbor. This linear form reflects the general pattern of the Navy Yard's industrial structures: a series of long, narrow buildings perpendicular to the shoreline. At the southern end of the building, a five-story, copper-roofed tower terminates the ensemble in a celebratory gesture. This cylindrical tower, which hints at the forms of seaside lighthouses, resolves the geometry of the street with the water's edge.

Uniform materials, window treatments, and special elements, like a brick water table and a continuous checkerboard stripe at the second story, tie the three masses together. The rowhouses vary in size from one-bedroom units (750 square feet) to four-bedroom units (1,500 square feet). Many of the residences have private balconies or outdoor spaces; furthermore, 47 of the 50 units have waterfront views. In the future, the rear parking area will become a child play area for the complex.

In addition to the Bricklayers and Laborers Non-Profit Housing Corporation, the City of Boston and the Boston Redevelopment Authority actively supported the project. Built at only $67 per square foot, the rowhouses were open to Boston residents at prices far below Boston's median housing costs, among the highest in the nation. The final product, completed in 1988, demonstrates that affordable housing can exist comfortably even in an expensive residential neighborhood.

Connecting Charlestown's main street
with the harbor, a seven-story structure
was created to extend the pattern of
linear gable-ended forms running
perpendicular from First Avenue to the
water (facing page, top). Forty-seven of
the 50 units have waterfront views
(facing page, bottom left). A five-story
cylindrical form marks the water's edge
(facing page, bottom right).

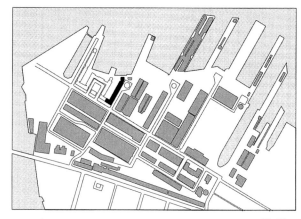

Site Plan

Plan Diagram: Structure

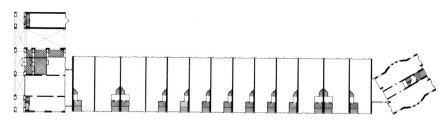

Plan Diagram: Structure, Access

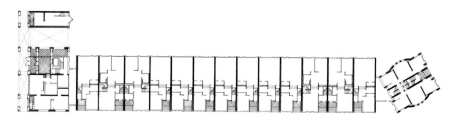

Plan Diagram: Structure, Access, Interior Walls

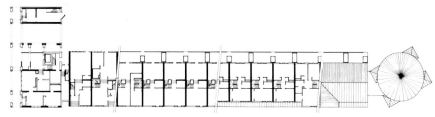

Plan Diagram: 1st Floor, 2nd Floor, 3rd Floor, Roof

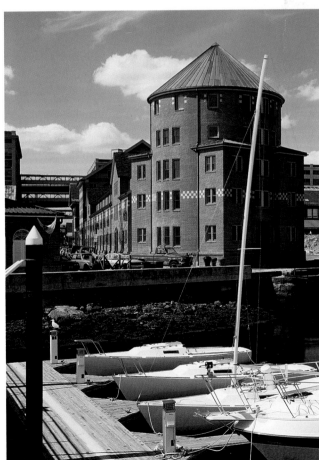

The building, with its three-part massing and large portal, creates an active relationship between the harbor and the city.

Rochester Riverfront Redevelopment
Rochester, New York
1986-1998

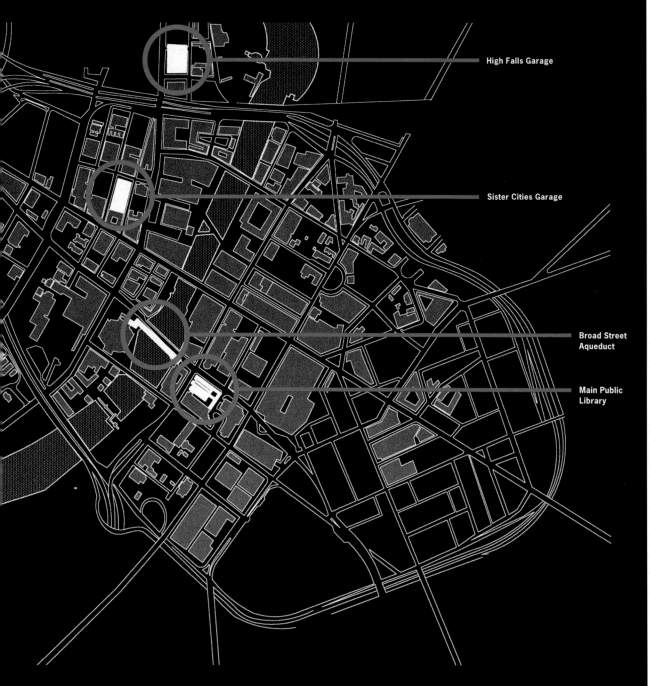

High Falls Garage

Sister Cities Garage

Broad Street
Aqueduct

Main Public
Library

City of Rochester: Ten Years of City-Building

Over a 15-year period, William Rawn Associates has played an important role in strengthening the downtown core of Rochester, New York, and assisting the city's efforts to combat suburban flight. The firm's work has revitalized three sectors of the downtown area: the Cultural District, the City Hall District, and the Library District. It has also generated the expansion of the High Falls Entertainment District. Their work is postulated on the idea that an architecture conceived as "city-building" engages the primary forms of the city: the street, the river, the bridges, and its industrial past.

Sister Cities Garage:
Rebuilding the Urban Fabric Opposite City Hall 1990

The 1,000-car Sister Cities Parking Garage was designed in the late 1980s as a civic building befitting its strategic location directly across from City Hall. The garage's street fronts recapture the brick patterns and metal rooflines of the neighborhood buildings. A series of pyramidal towers along the garage's exterior echo the massing atop City Hall and the older buildings surrounding it. Stores along the ground floor of the garage create street activity, animating the block and encouraging further development on surrounding sites.

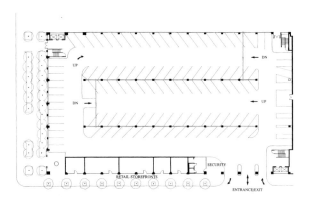

Ground Floor Plan

Rochester Riverfront Zoning Guidelines
Reconnecting the City to the River
1992

In order to direct the revitalization of the downtown waterfront district along the Genesee River, the 1992 Riverfront Zoning Guidelines take advantage of Rochester's unique status as one of the few American cities that straddles its river. These guidelines employed strategies to ensure that major streets, parallel to and one block back from the water on both banks, would be physically and visually connected to the Genesee River. A more fluid connection to the river allows these streets and the greater city to participate in the revitalization generated by the riverfront. The zoning guidelines established during this project were incorporated into the city's zoning code.

The centerpiece of the proposal was the conversion of the unused historic Broad Street Aqueduct, located over the Genesee River, into a pedestrian route and enclosed year-round urban park. The architects used a "bridge-as-building" concept to stitch the city together across the river. As a pedestrian promenade, the aqueduct would link the two sides of the city, even in the harsh Rochester winter. The southern half of the aqueduct would be an indoor park with glazed walls and roof; by contrast, the northern half would be an exterior waterway that could carry barges in the summer or hold an ice skating rink in the winter. On the upper level of the aqueduct would be three lanes of auto traffic, narrowed from the bridge's existing six lanes.

Site Plan

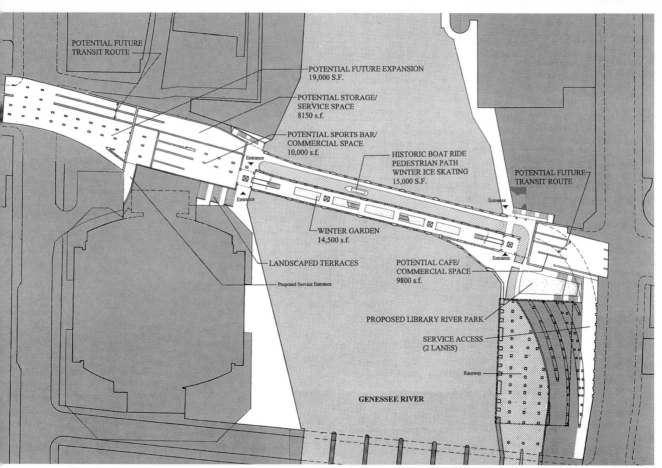

POTENTIAL FUTURE
TRANSIT ROUTE

POTENTIAL FUTURE EXPANSION
19,000 S.F.

POTENTIAL STORAGE/
SERVICE SPACE
8150 s.f.

POTENTIAL SPORTS BAR/
COMMERCIAL SPACE
10,000 s.f.

HISTORIC BOAT RIDE
PEDESTRIAN PATH
WINTER ICE SKATING
15,000 S.F.

POTENTIAL FUTURE
TRANSIT ROUTE

Entrance

Entrance

Entrance

WINTER GARDEN
14,500 s.f.

LANDSCAPED TERRACES

POTENTIAL CAFE/
COMMERCIAL SPACE
9800 s.f.

Proposed Service Entrance

PROPOSED LIBRARY RIVER PARK

SERVICE ACCESS
(2 LANES)

Raceway

GENESSEE RIVER

Lower Level Plan of Aqueduct

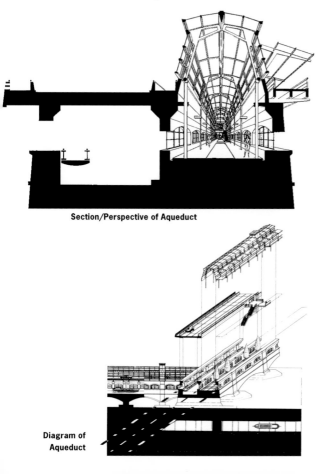

Section/Perspective of Aqueduct

**Diagram of
Aqueduct**

Perspective of Aqueduct

High Falls Garage:
A Gateway to the New Entertainment District 1994

The seven-level High Falls Parking Garage is the centerpiece of a revitalization strategy in Rochester's historic Brown's Race neighborhood, an industrial area along the Genesee River. The nine million dollar project contains parking for 750 cars as well as street-level retail space.

The garage reinterprets the neighborhood's industrial palette—steel, concrete, and masonry—with high-tech and urban-scaled forms. A 100-foot exterior stair tower, which marks the garage's southwest corner, serves as a beacon, announcing a new entertainment district to the city. Continuously projected light on the underside screens of the tower top celebrates the role of high technology in Rochester and acknowledges the Kodak world headquarters across the street. A triangular brick base supports a free-standing pedestrian bridge over the garage entrance. Proof of the garage's contribution to the revitalized neighborhood, a new minor-league baseball stadium was built within sight of the garage, due in part to the liveliness of the garage's design.

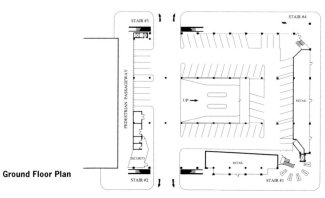

Ground Floor Plan

Main Public Library: *An Urban Connector* 1998

The $26 million, 100,000-square-foot new Main Public Library building is located across South Avenue from Rochester's original Beaux-Arts main public library. The design establishes a new urban library typology that celebrates openness, accessibility, and direct connection to the city. An interior street runs through the heart of the library, a four-story skylit atrium conceived as a civic space. Colorful bridges span the atrium, connecting the two long, narrow bars that comprise each floor. These bridges are deliberately non-aligned to maintain the spatial integrity of the continuous 200-foot-long atrium. Two main entrances at the ends of the long atrium space connect the city's midtown shopping area with the Genesee riverfront.

The ground floor celebrates a strong visual connection to the city with a large periodicals reading room along the street. The long bars flanking the atrium on the upper floors organize reference desks for each floor in the southern bar with the reading areas and open stacks in the northern bar.

Each face of Fire Station No. 6
contains different patterns of
glass, giving the building a distinct
iconography from each side.

Columbus Fire Station No. 6
Columbus, Indiana
1998

In a long line of famous Columbus fire stations, such as the Leighton Bowers–designed Station No.1 and the Venturi & Rauch–designed Station No.4, Fire Station No.6 stands as a contemporary civic icon designed specifically for the fast-moving rural highway in the southern sector of Columbus.

The fire station is a simple glass, stone, and brick structure with an undulating roof profile created by a series of curved steel trusses. Recognizing that the so-called side façades are more visible to the passing motorists, the architects developed the east and west sides as "fronts" which boast two distinct glass grids: one formed by the trio of glass garage doors, the other formed by the glass block infill.

The south elevation, fronting the highway, is clad in a solid skin of concrete masonry that resembles stone. This façade also incorporates a continuous four-foot-high horizontal strip window. By day, the glass block takes on the same coloration as the stone; at night, the building becomes a beacon, as its glass and glass block elevations glow from within. The structure responds to the Kevin Roche–designed Cummins Midrange Engine Plant at Walesboro, a stark, luminous glass box located a half-mile west.

Attached to the small roadside pavilion is a long brick-clad bar building that houses a garage, a service room, bedrooms, and a kitchen. The building is a protective presence to the growing neighborhoods nearby. Its iconic quality is so strong that it was selected as the graphic representation of the southern part of town in Columbus' new mapping system.

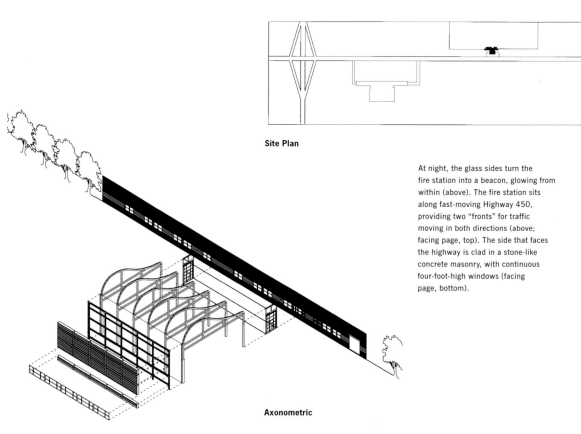

Site Plan

Axonometric

At night, the glass sides turn the fire station into a beacon, glowing from within (above). The fire station sits along fast-moving Highway 450, providing two "fronts" for traffic moving in both directions (above; facing page, top). The side that faces the highway is clad in a stone-like concrete masonry, with continuous four-foot-high windows (facing page, bottom).

When complete, the tall, slim glass
form of the Loews Boston Hotel will
stand as an integral part of Boston's
Theater District skyline.

Loews Boston Hotel
Boston Theater District, Boston, Massachusetts 2002

Through an architecture of contemporary minimalism at an urban scale, the Loews Boston Hotel demonstrates how an urban hotel can capture the "democracy of the street" in downtown Boston's Theater District.

The tall, thin form of the Loews Boston Hotel, an intentional departure from the block-shaped slab of most conventional hotels, is achieved by the juxtaposition of two slender components: an all-glass sliver and a metal-paneled sliver. The all-glass form faces north and incorporates long views of the city; the second form, combining both metal and glass, faces south. Continuous, acute, vertical corners at the ends of the all-glass element further accentuate the hotel's thinness, especially when it is viewed from the east or west. These acute corners, which are back-lit for most of the day, will appear transparent when viewed from important parts of the city, giving the building a distinct skyline presence with its vertical edges.

A second major defining element of the building is its taut glass façade, which reinforces the building's openness and connection to the city. From atop the 25-story tower, guests will have sweeping views of Boston Common and the Public Garden, the Back Bay neighborhood, the Massachusetts State House, and the city's financial district. Clear glass creates a direct visual connection between the street and the hotel's major public spaces, including the lobby, lounge, and restaurant; consequently, the public spaces animate the pedestrian experience and indeed capture the "democracy of the street" in Boston. The entire building has a series of faceted planes. Four major facets mark the tower. This faceted clear glass façade oscillates between reflection and transparency, depending on the time of day, the weather conditions, and the angle at which the building is viewed. The facets give the hotel a dynamic presence appropriate to the Theater District, allowing the building's shape to change as the viewer moves around it.

The hotel's angular glass form, rising from the street plane, will be visible throughout the city, signaling "the crossroads of the Theater District" with its distinct crystalline form. Another feature for the urban hotel will be a new 31,000-square-foot Performance Development Center facility with its own street-level entrance, built for nearby Emerson College. Three large "black box" theater spaces will replicate the size of the Emerson Majestic Theater's stage, where many of the city's non-profit theater groups perform.

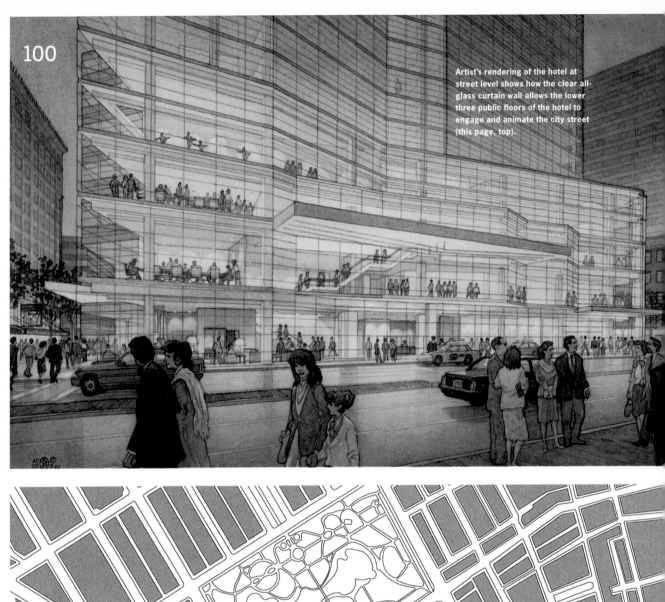

Artist's rendering of the hotel at street level shows how the clear all-glass curtain wall allows the lower three public floors of the hotel to engage and animate the city street (this page, top).

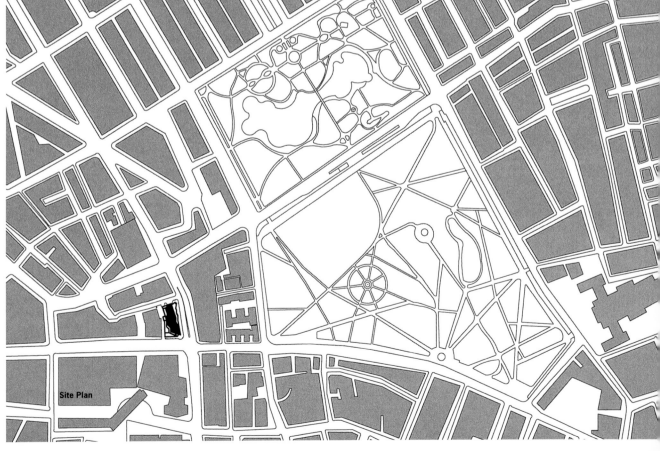

Site Plan

As seen in these computer-generated views of the hotel, the glass facets and sharp corners of this 25-story glass tower create a dynamic marker at the epicenter of the Theater District.

Campus an

d the City

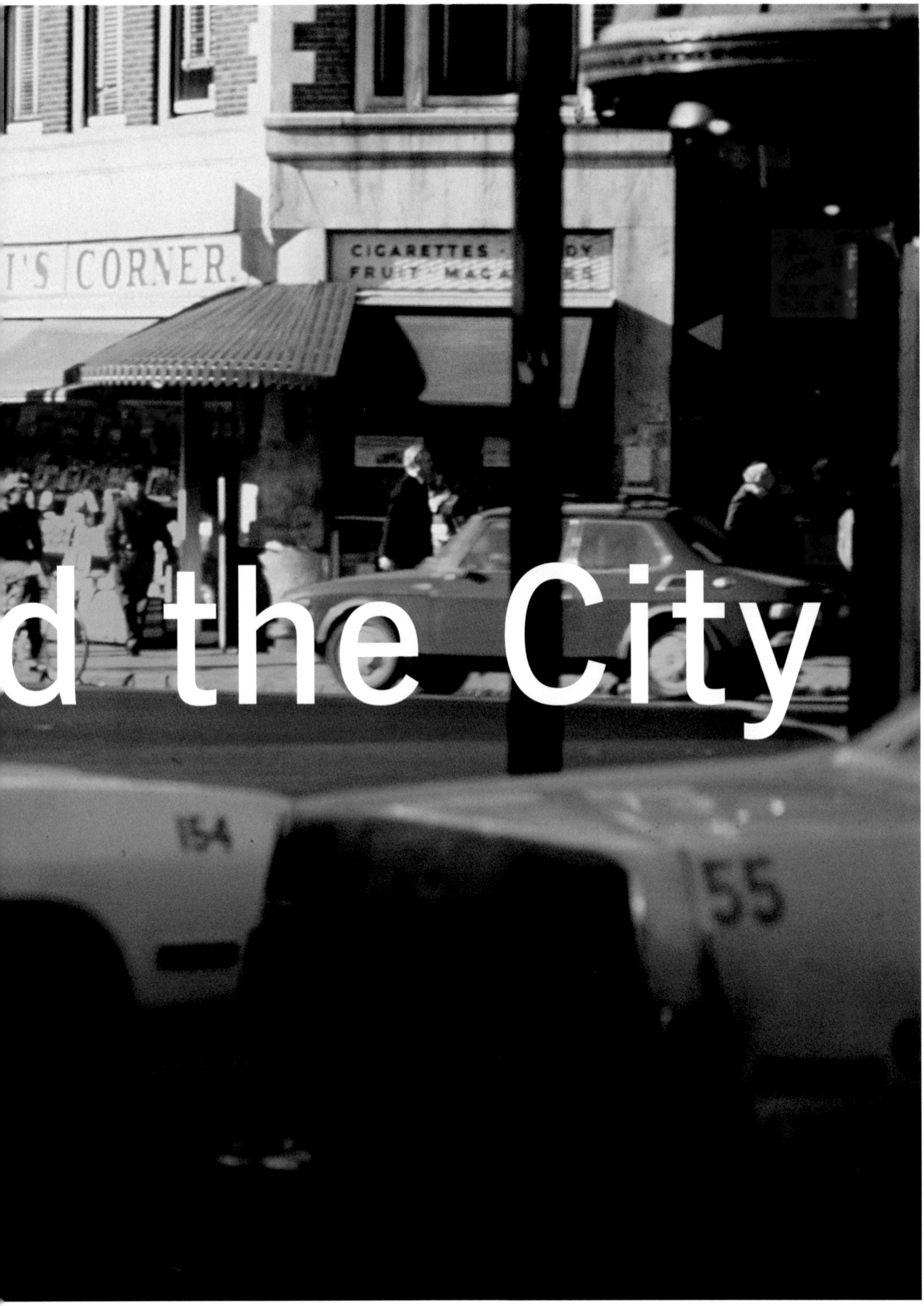

Campus and the City
by William Rawn

Based on a lecture given at Boston's Museum of Fine Arts on February 24, 1999

Boston's late 20th-century renaissance is based on a mix of physical, cultural, and economic forces that are generated by the universities and colleges permeating the life of the city. There are special social and economic connections between the city and its universities that warrant celebration. But this suggests that there might be a special architectural connection between the city and its universities as well. Are there elements of this physical connection that can generate even more positive qualities for the city and the university in the future? Richard Freeland, president of Northeastern college campuses, nor will it explore its fundamental differences from the continental European urban model. Earliest colleges were located in cities (William & Mary, Harvard), followed by colleges founded on the frontier (Williams, Dartmouth), followed later by land grant universities located in semi-rural settings, followed still later by late 19th-century universities located quite far from even a small town (Stanford, Duke, Rice). Only in the late 20th century has there been a rise (I hesitate to call it a resurgence) of the campus located in the city: individual campuses (e.g. Boston University, Northeastern, NYU, Temple,

University, has outlined the defining academic and social goals for his urban university, goals which are indeed based on an intense interaction with Boston, its host city.

Our daily encounter with the benefits of a city closely integrated with its colleges and universities has inspired our campus work across the country. In most settings, we try to reinforce the positive influences that cities and towns have on their universities, and vice versa. We constantly ask the central question about the nature of this relationship: How can one translate a city's urbanity into an architecture of urbanity for its universities? At their best, campuses extend influence beyond their confines, affecting and enriching the cities and towns around them. At their worst, they can be isolated and isolating.

This lecture does not seek to review the rich and fascinating history of American

Georgetown, George Washington) and a set of newer state university campuses, usually secondary to the main "downstate" campus (e.g. University of Illinois at Chicago Circle, University of Wisconsin at Madison, University of Massachusetts at Boston).

One can posit that urban campuses gain from economic, cultural, and social involvement with the city, and from interaction with the day-to-day life of the city. Can the campus, in fact, learn more from the complexity, confusion, drama, and subtlety of the city? And can the city gain from the presence of an increasingly worldly and sophisticated campus?

If the answer to both questions is yes, how then can city and campus create physical forms that generate and foster these mutual advantages? Are students better prepared to cope with the complexities of a 21st-century economy coming from a city experience? And in the age of the multinational economy, are these students better able to deal with the complexities of the global economy?

To understand these opportunities, specific characteristics of an urban campus warrant recognition: 1) The physical connection of campus buildings to the city buildings nearby; 2) The coherent relationship of the campus to the city street system, and the ease with which streets and pedestrian paths pass through the campus; 3) The seamlessness of the line where the campus ends and the city begins; 4) The relative openness of the campus to the city and vice versa; 5) The integra-

In this quiet, green campus space, formed by individual buildings with a strong sense of edge, an interaction takes place between the citizens and the students that is intense and constant. This space is public because a continuous wall of buildings does not bind it; it is a campus because the buildings nonetheless create a sharply defined green space.

Yale University is analogous though different. Early buildings were organized to face the New Haven Green, and became part of the Green. Over three centuries, Yale started building

tion of residential, academic, and student life activities throughout the campus, a decidedly urban concept, as opposed to the separation of such campus functions in highly separate precincts; and 6) The relative proportion of buildings and open space on the campus, and how that relates to the density of the surrounding city.

Let me propose that we can divide universities into three types when examining the relationship between city and campus. The first model is the campus closely connected to its city, indeed, seamlessly connected to its city.

For this model, one might ask, what would Harvard University be without Harvard Square? Harvard Square is obviously a vibrant retail center. But what fascinates me about Harvard Square is actually Harvard Yard: namely, how the citizens of Cambridge, non-students coming to and from the Square, are constantly traversing the Yard.

walls around itself. Its Residential Colleges, built shortly after the River Houses at Harvard in the 1930s, walled themselves off from the city in a very assertive way. Yet other parts of the Yale campus, like the Cross Campus, are open to the life of the city. The newer parts of Yale, located at the university's edges, relate more seamlessly to the city. Louis Kahn's extraordinary design for the Yale Center for British Art locates the museum above the stores of Chapel Street. This produces a continuing connection between campus and city, as well as a profound connection between a great building and the city.

At the University of Pennsylvania, Locust Walk, once a city street and now the central pedestrian path on campus, collects pedestrian movement to create a powerful place of university community. Walnut Street, just one block away, defines an edge of campus and, formerly, had no such vitality. Now, though, the university has wisely sought to strengthen Walnut Street's urban quality with a series of four- and five-story buildings, which house retail on the ground level and university facilities on the upper stories. This initiative will develop a deeper connection between campus and city, helping the university to break out of its former defensive mentality. Similar initiatives are occurring in several other precincts of this campus as the university starts to create a meaningful physical dialogue with its West Philadelphia neighborhood.

The successful campus-city connection need not be limited to campuses in big cities. One of the most seamless connections between city and campus occurs at Dartmouth College in Hanover, New Hampshire. The Hanover Green, which is without question a public place, faces the campus buildings in a way that forces one to traverse across this public space to get from one part of campus to another. Likewise, Hopkins Center, Nelson Rockefeller's great gift to his alma mater, is located where the Green and Main Street meet. With its art, music, and theater

Even if a university is located in the middle of a city, it may not achieve that seamless connection. In Hartford, Connecticut, Trinity College's "Long Walk" is one of the most beautiful Collegiate Gothic buildings in the country. Yet this building forms a strong urban wall, a wall that protects the campus and its green space ambiance, which is totally different from that of the city surrounding it. Now, our office, with a team of other architects, has developed a master plan that covers not only the campus, but also the city around it. It is a plan based on the establishment of careful yet strong connections between city and campus. Our design for the Summit Residence Halls refers to the strong linear forms of the Long Walk. And yet, to establish a direct connection between city and campus, it provides a major portal to the street plus a campus-defining—and city-defining—tower as the southern entry to the campus.

offerings frequented by townspeople, and with its all-important student mailboxes ensuring undergraduates' interaction with adjacent Main Street, Hopkins Center is literally a link to the world beyond the edge of campus.

A second model of the relationship between campus and city is the campus that is located next to a city or town but remains somewhat separate from it. The University of Virginia, located at the edge of Charlottesville, is one example. Thomas Jefferson purposely founded the University of Virginia nearly two miles from the City of Charlottesville. It is ironic that the location of the new University had a decidedly anti-urban bias, because the architectural design of the Lawn, Jefferson's centerpiece of the University, is a decidedly urban structure.

In 1992, John Casteen, President of the University of Virginia wanted to know, "Why is the university always moving in a suburban direction when it is adjacent to such a lively small city? What can be done to improve its urban sensibility?" The University of Virginia and the City of Charlottesville jointly hired our firm to create an urban design plan that would improve the somewhat dilapidated and empty West Main Street Corridor that connects the university to downtown.

The year-long project included sometimes contentious—and often quite wonderful—community meetings. Ultimately, the City Council approved the plan and invited the univer-

campuses are extraordinarily beautiful. Yet connections to their nearby cities are negligible. A more recent example is the new SUNY campus at Purchase in New York state, a university dedicated to the arts (and what should be more closely connected to the city than the arts?). The campus is located in the far suburbs of Westchester County, surrounded by lush green fields and isolated from any city.

Stanford University is also isolated from its host city, with the center of Stanford's campus located a mile and a half from downtown

sity to move eastward toward the city for the first time in 100 years. The plan proposed three residential colleges for the university, community-based middle income housing serving the nearby African-American neighborhoods, community facilities, major commercial facilities around the railroad station, and community-based commercial buildings for the neighborhood. For the residential colleges, we developed a set of building models that captured the essence of a Jefferson-inspired university, but placed those buildings in decidedly urban locations. The city has implemented the plan, and development is occurring as the plan envisioned.

The third model of the campus is a far more common one: the campus that is totally unconnected to the city around it. Duke University, Stanford University, and, to an extent, Rice University are ideal examples of this type. Physically, these

Palo Alto. Try to walk to a neighborhood drugstore or record store when you are on the Stanford campus; there are none. There are other aspects of Stanford that are absolutely exceptional such as the quality of education and the elegance of its architecture. But the elements of city or town life, including retail and commercial choices and connections to a non-campus world, do not exist near the day-to-day life of the campus.

The same could be said of Duke University. The Gothic campus, powerful as an architecture, sits surrounded by the woods, a couple miles from the active life of Durham, North Carolina. That isolation sets a very different tone for the campus. While the center may be quite beautiful, the campus reflects an almost suburban, car-dominated pattern of organization.

In addition to the exploration of these campus models, it is important to recognize

Aerial view of Boston, highlighting the Northeastern University campus located between the high spine of Back Bay and the cultural institutions of the Fenway, including the Museum of Fine Arts. The new west campus is at the bottom of the image, next to playing fields and sited on a former parking lot.

that urbanity applies also to the nature of the buildings themselves and how they relate to the adjacent city pattern of buildings and streets. One building type is a "wall" that clearly defines the campus edge, like the one created by the Harvard Houses or the Yale Colleges. These usually imply a sharp demarcation between campus and city. Another is the condition where buildings frame a space accessible to the city, such as the buildings at Harvard Yard. These buildings have small or large open spaces between them, welcoming the city to enter the campus. A third building type is where buildings form a well-

lots to its ever-expanding periphery. That policy runs the risk of forever separating a campus from its surrounding community. Increasingly, this growth model is becoming politically untenable, architecturally dreary, and urbanistically self-defeating. In Northeastern's case, the university ran out of available open land.

In designing the three new residence halls, we created walled buildings that form a strong interior quadrangle; the walls are then punctured with two oversized portals (each 30 feet wide, and four and three stories high, respectively). The

defined green space, opening toward the street. The best examples are those open spaces that are framed by strong-edged buildings that lock the sense of campus to the street.

When our firm began master planning work for the West Campus of Northeastern University, a new sector of this urban campus facing a major city boulevard (Huntington Avenue) and the Museum of Fine Arts in Boston, we sought to address two important issues. First, we undertook an urban design study of the university along Huntington Avenue, making recommendations for particular buildings that reinforce the sense of this major commercial boulevard as the most important face of the campus. This stance generated the basic design of the first three West Campus buildings.

Second, like many larger universities in urban or suburban settings, Northeastern has traditionally grown by simply moving its parking

portals have no gates and the views they offer give a sense of a green respite in the city. These portals state very clearly that the public is welcome into the campus, in support of Northeastern's long-time policy of openness to the city, a policy that emanates from its earlier days as a commuter institution. This solution, in effect, merges at least two of the campus building types cited above.

The West Campus is a highly permeable, open construct; it's not the tight-walled buildings of the Harvard houses. The largest portal aligns with Museum Road on the other side of Huntington Avenue, further accentuating that the building is open to the city and the city's street grid across the boulevard. Likewise, the second portal is aligned in a different direction to face Huntington Avenue. In addition, the complex has a 13-story tower that acts as an anchor and a beacon for the quadrangle.

We used glass selectivity to celebrate visual connections to the city. On the ground floor, we created student activity spaces with floor-to-ceiling windows; these spaces are designed to activate and enliven the street edge and the street life at the city side of these buildings. The use of floor-to-ceiling glass for the living rooms on the building's corners adds another sense of openness and transparency to an otherwise dominantly brick building. The Phase II buildings added a pair of eight-story elements, made completely of a floor-to-ceiling glass wall that acts as another welcoming city. It is only with a strong city and a strong campus that the two entities in effect become one. The urbanity and the resultant urban sensibility will bring strength to both the city and the campus, acknowledging that the campus and its students gain much from the city, just as the city gains much from the campus. That, in the end, is the goal.

(31) Harvard University
(32) Williams College
(33) Williams College
(34) Harvard University
(35) Yale University
(36) Yale University

(46) Northeastern University: View of urban-scaled quad
(47) Northeastern University: View up Huntington Avenue
(48) Northeastern University: Aerial view

threshold to the complex from the east. The six-story datum for most of the building refers to the five- and six-story buildings of the surrounding Fenway neighborhood, while the 13-story tower relates to the taller buildings that march along Huntington Avenue from downtown.

In the master plan, we posited the possibility that Northeastern could join with the Wentworth Institute of Technology (an adjacent institution) to create a permanent green open space facing Huntington Avenue and the Museum of Fine Arts. It could become a major civic space, a literal Town Common, for this section of Boston, further cementing the connections of these three institutions to the life and rhythm of the city.

These campus-making techniques will ensure that the Northeastern campus is simultaneously meeting its campus needs and pursuing city-making strategies that strengthen the adjacent

(37) University of Pennsylvania
(38) Dartmouth College
(39) University of Virginia
(40) University of Virginia
(41) Stanford University
(42) Yale University
(43) Northeastern University: Aerial view
(44) Northeastern University: Aerial view
(45) Northeastern University: View along Parker Street

In 1992, William Rawn Associates developed a scheme that included a large entry tower, several large gallery spaces, and a second-level sculpture garden overlooking the street (facing page, top). The 1989 scheme incorporated a large subway station into the museum, placing art and video monitors throughout the station to intertwine the city with the ICA (facing page, bottom).

Institute of Contemporary Art
Boston, Massachusetts 1989, 1992

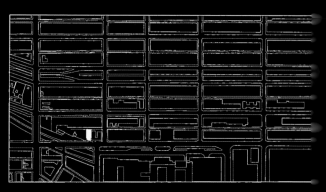

Site Plan

Two projects for the Institute of Contemporary Art (ICA) expand the possibilities of a contemporary art museum in a populist, democratic city by redefining the boundaries between museum and city, between art and information.

In 1989, William Rawn Associates developed a plan for a new 40,000-square-foot home for the ICA on a site adjacent to its existing building in Boston's Back Bay. The plan proposed integrating the ICA into a large hotel and office complex, using air rights over the Massachusetts Turnpike and taking advantage of direct access to a nearby subway station. After the 1989 project was put on hold, the architects made a more modest proposal in 1992 for renovating the existing ICA building and adding new facilities on an adjacent site.

The 1989 scheme challenges traditional boundaries—drawing the city inward and expanding the museum outward. The proposal allowed the museum lobby to include a major subway entrance and placed museum artwork and museum video monitors throughout the subway station. The collision between museum and city would create new opportunities for contemporary art to interact with this multicultural, multi-economic upper–Boylston Street crossroads of Boston.

The 1992 scheme, by reinterpreting the strong history between great museums and great streets, continues to challenge traditional museum boundaries. An entry tower that incorporates an urban-scaled video screen, a sculpture garden overlooking the street, and a street-level café combine to transform the sidewalk and street into an open museum gallery.

The entry tower of the 1992 scheme incorporates an enormous video screen and a street-level café that brings the city into the building and the museum into the city.

Lively discussion at one of many
community meetings around a 15-
foot-long model of the development
plan for this one mile corridor
between the University of Virginia
and downtown Charlottesville.

West Main Street Corridor Urban Design Plan

University of Virginia and City of Charlottesville, Charlottesville, Virginia 1993

This urban design plan explores the relationship between university and city at the very place that established the nature of "town and gown" in the American consciousness.

West Main Street is perhaps the archetype for American streets which connect universities and their host cities. In 1825, Thomas Jefferson deliberately located his university a mile from the city of Charlottesville. Over 175 years, that mile-long road has evolved; sadly, decay, empty stores, and vacant lots mark its most recent 25 years.

The project employs an "incremental growth" strategy to integrate one million square feet of development into a continuous, modestly scaled streetscape. The plan proposes three new residential colleges for 1,000 students, plus community facilities, such as shops, a recreation center, a park, 70 units of housing, a medical hotel, a new train station connection to West Main Street, and new parking.

The architects created a new residence hall typology to generate an urban form appropriate to Charlottesville. This design applies the ideas of Jefferson's "Academical Village" to a decidedly urban setting. It engages West Main Street without overwhelming it: the three- and four-story building elements, with street-level retail, create an active street edge while maintaining the public open space traditions of the university.

Charlottesville's City Council approved the plan in 1993. For the first time in a century, the city invited the university to expand along West Main Street toward its downtown. The city uses the project to define future growth along the corridor.

Residential College in a Semi-Rural Setting

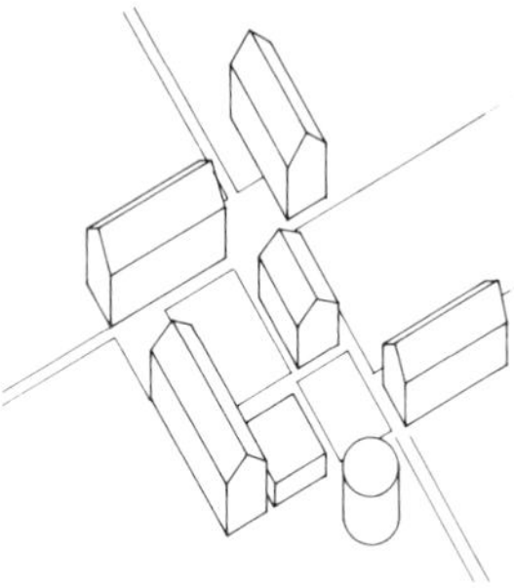

Prototype

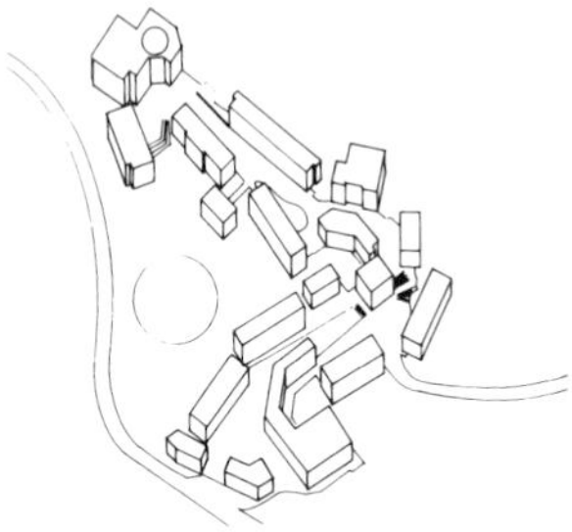

UC Santa Cruz: Kresge College

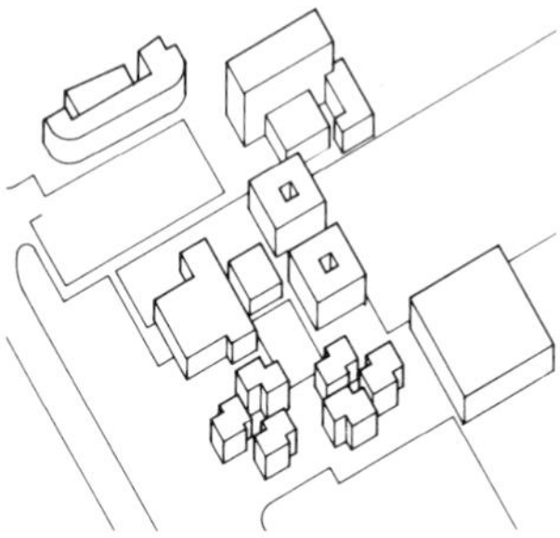

UC San Diego: Revelle College

Charlottesville: Residential College in a Small Town

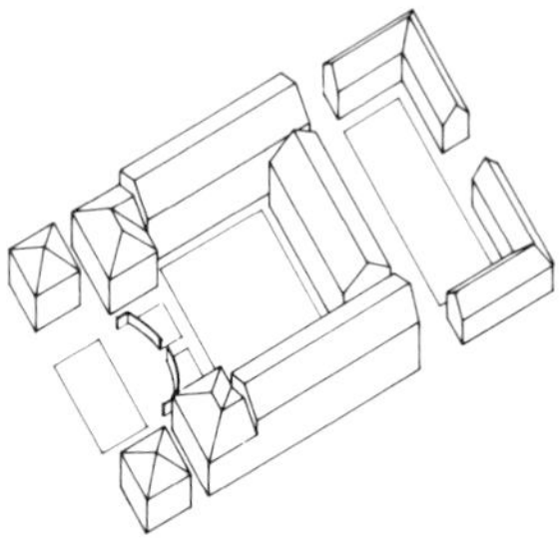

West Main Street Prototype

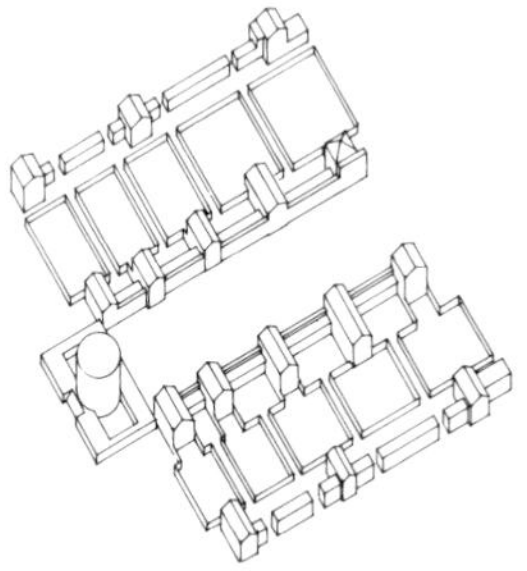

University of Virginia: The Lawn

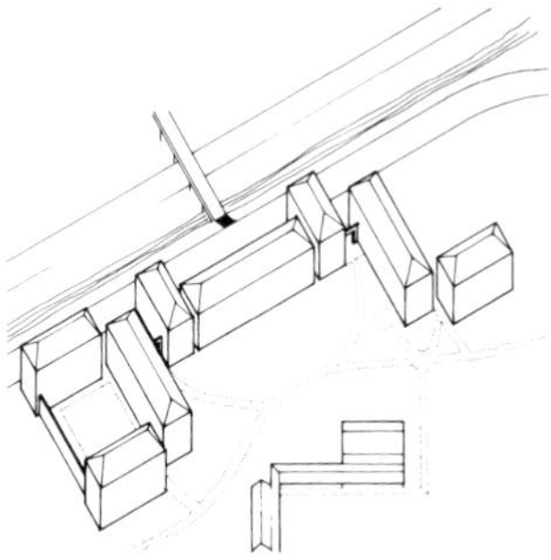

Monroe Hill

Residential College in an Urban Setting

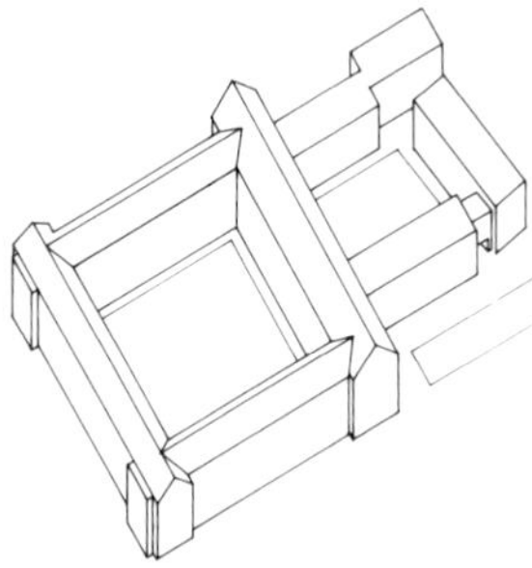

Prototype

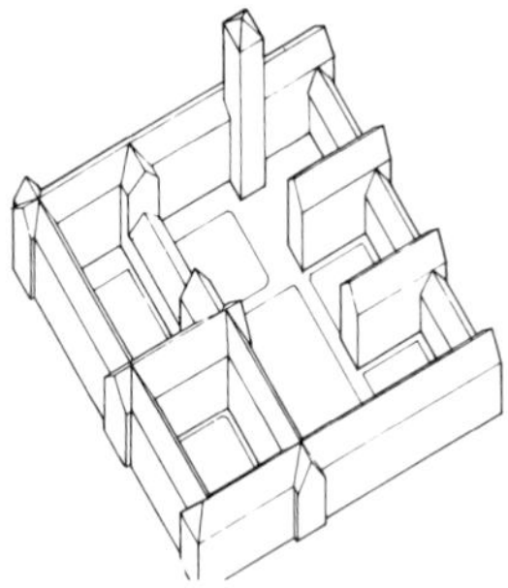

Yale: Saybrook and Branford Colleges

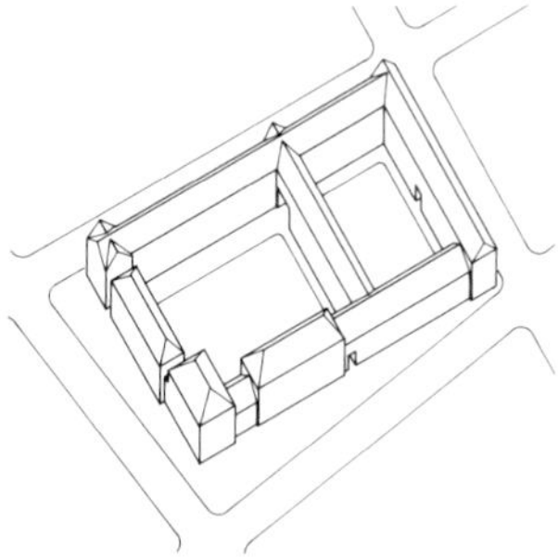

Harvard: Lowell House

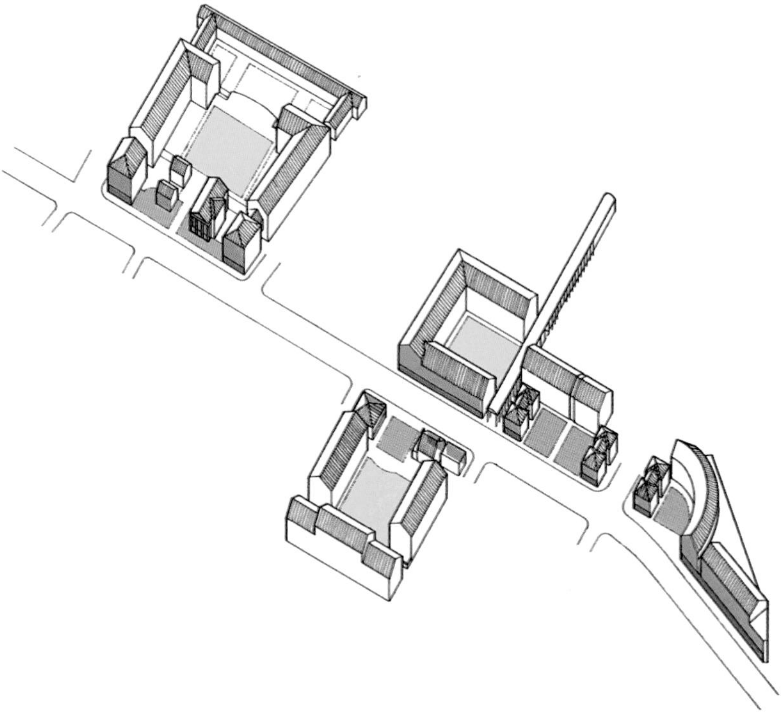

Axonometric: Three Residential Colleges

Artist's rendering of a future Residential College along West Main Street that creates a strong and active street edge while maintaining open public spaces (above).

Views into Semi-Private Outdoor Space

FACULTY HOUSING
- Overlooks Street
- Defines Public Open Space along Street
- Forms Gateway into College

STUDY/MEETING AREA
- Defines Public Open Space along Street
- Incorporates Existing Historic Structure into Typology

DORMITORY ROOM
- Overlooks Street

DINING COMMON
- Overlooks Street

RETAIL
- Along Street

Axonometirc: Detail Along Street Edge

A strong circular form creates a
dynamic open space connecting the
major pedestrian spine, Locust
Walk, with active city streets, Walnut
and 40th Streets (facing page, top).
Each Residence Hall features its
own iconic five-story glass entry
tower (facing page, bottom).

Superblock Housing Competition
University of Pennsylvania, Philadelphia, Pennsylvania 1999

This competition entry for new housing for 1,600 students posits a new relationship between the university and the city, one that reverses the university's history of looking inward rather than outward.

The existing Superblock at the University of Pennsylvania, a four square, 21-acre site (bounded by Spruce, Walnut, 38th, and 40th Streets) that contains an awkward collection of low- and mid-rise buildings and three 24-story towers, is unique in its failings. It feels detached from the rest of the university and it conspicuously separates itself from the surrounding city.

The architects proposed a strong circular open space, formed by five-story buildings, to bring the campus and the city together. This major public open space at the western end of Locust Walk strengthens the walk as the primary pedestrian spine, organizing the campus and acting as a major gateway between the campus and the corner of Walnut and 40th Street, a corner that is evolving as a major campus-city crossroads. The strong spatial qualities of this significant urban form stand up to the size and scalelessness of the existing Superblock.

The architects also proposed nine new residence halls, using a new typology they developed for college housing at the university: an intensely urban structure that fosters a smaller academic community within the university. Iconic gateway elements and dedicated outdoor space define each of the individual residence halls. Each hall contains a glazed five-story entrance block with shared functions, such as lounges, exercise areas, libraries, and study spaces, which are decidedly urban spaces. Public functions on the ground floors—shops, a city library, and a theater—tie the buildings to West Philadelphia's economic and civic life.

Nine Residence Halls, with nine distinct entry towers, redefine the Superblock around a network of open spaces.

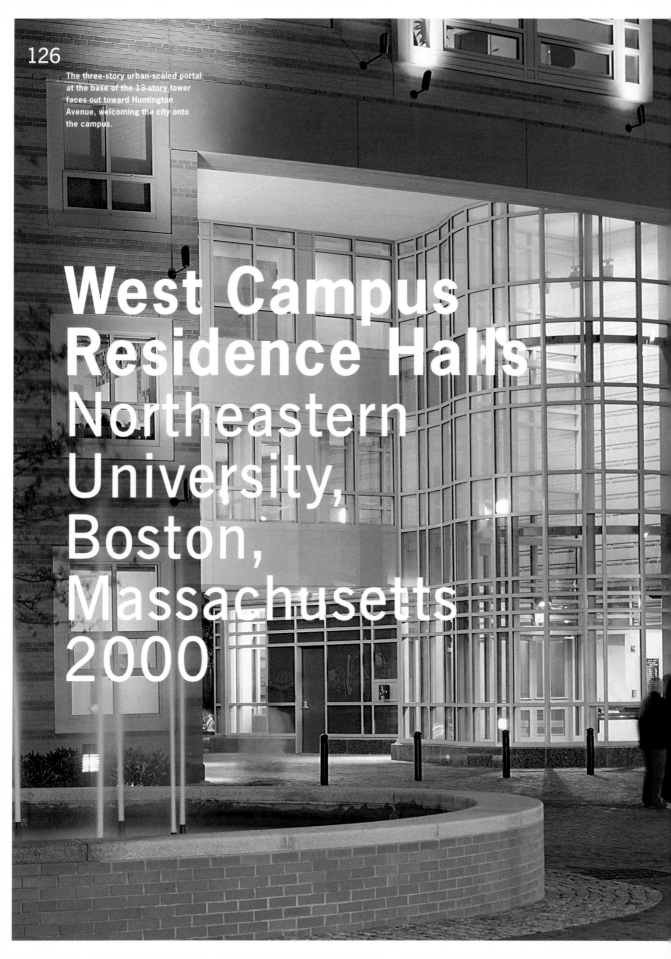

The three-story urban-scaled portal at the base of the 13-story tower faces out toward Huntington Avenue, welcoming the city onto the campus.

West Campus Residence Halls
Northeastern University, Boston, Massachusetts 2000

In order to reinforce this urban university's connection to the city and adjacent major cultural institutions, this project transforms the residence hall into a civic building—adapting an age-old typology to explicitly open up the campus to the city.

The West Campus Residence Halls at Northeastern University, a $64 million, 400,000-square-foot complex for 1,050 students, comprise the first phase of the West Campus Master Plan developed by William Rawn Associates to organize a ten-acre site with 1.2 million gross square feet of new facilities. Five major architectural gestures mark these residence halls: a 13-story tower, two large portals, two glass gatepost elements, a sinuous building form, and an urban-scaled public quadrangle.

The 13-story tower presents the new West Campus to the city and to one of the city's preeminent cultural boulevards, Huntington Avenue. With its strong curved shape, the building has a dynamic presence in the city. The design creates a different profile at each view corridor.

Two large portals (one four and a half stories, the other three stories) in the building's western façade mark the main entrances to the new West Campus. These urban-scaled portals open up a strong street wall and define powerful thresholds that dramatically open the campus to the city. Building entrances located in each portal orient the complex to both the city and the campus simultaneously.

The complex features two eight-story, all-glass tower elements. These towers serve as urban gateposts, signaling the threshold of a future main pedestrian promenade that will connect the new urban quadrangle with an existing academic area and a major subway station. They reinforce the public nature of the new West Campus and coordinate with the portals to frame views between the city and the campus.

Sinuous and undulating walls bind the building into a single form that stands up to the civic scale of two other major institutions, the Museum of Fine Arts and Wentworth Institute of Technology, located across an open green space. This simple use of sinuous curves, which reference gently curved Baroque façades or Alvar Aalto's Baker House at nearby MIT, brings a dynamic quality that animates the strong street edge, helps soften the building's mass, and accentuates the thin, vertical tower as it embraces a new quadrangle.

The three buildings form an open space that attracts students and neighboring residents alike. Among its many antecedents, the new urban-scaled quadrangle (150 x 200 feet) brings to mind Barcelona's Plaza Real, with its identical size and height, its analogous gatepost and portal elements, and its permeability to the city.

Public spaces on the ground floor face both the quadrangle and the city streets, integrating the campus into the fabric of the city. The ground floor also contains common areas, with separate meeting, study, television, and game rooms, as well as a mailroom and laundry facilities. Student apartments upstairs, typically for four students, feature fully equipped kitchens, living rooms, and private baths.

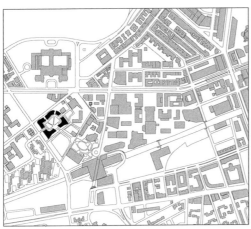

Site Plan

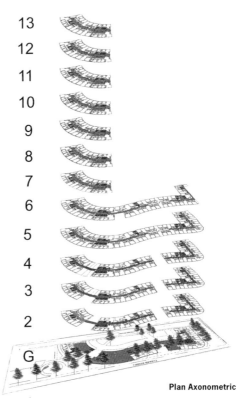

Plan Axonometric

The curved 13-story tower, as seen from Huntington Avenue, introduces the West Campus to the city (facing page). A sinuous building form embraces Parker Street and helps draw the city through the four-story portal onto campus (above, left). Two eight-story, all-glass towers serve as gateway elements between the new urban quad and a future academic corridor (above, right).

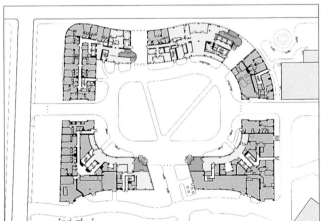

Ground Floor Plan

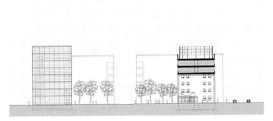

Site Section Through Quad Facing Northeast

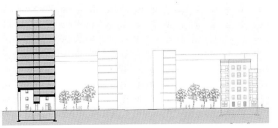

Site Section Through Quad Facing East

Taut detailing and clear glass create a strong sense of daytime transparency that complements the towers' nighttime glow (facing page, this page).

Wrapping around an interior quad, the curving buildings create a sense of campus identity while remaining open to the city (facing page, top). Transparent corners allow corner living rooms to take full advantage of city views (facing page, bottom left). Two portals—one at four stories (facing page, bottom right), one at three (this page)—form welcoming entrances to the West Campus.

The collection of four- and six-story
buildings fits comfortably into a
tight and sloping site.

The Summit Residence Complex and Court
Trinity College, Hartford, Connecticut 2000

An iconic tower, a long bar building, and an elevated plateau combine to create a modern counterpoint to the founding buildings on the Trinity College campus.

The Summit Residence Complex and Court accommodates 173 beds in four- and six-story buildings on the top of an open plinth or plateau—a powerful example of moderately large buildings that fit into a tight site. As the first set of buildings constructed under a new master plan, these residence halls demonstrate how a campus can increase its density while maintaining its existing campus texture.

The Summit Residences establish an appropriate architectural connection between William Burges' extraordinary Long Walk and the highly varied campus buildings constructed since 1960. A new long bar building, which includes a portal, anchors the project and the campus to the city, recalling Burges in a fundamentally modernist way. The interior building has a decidedly more sculptural form in plan, a more varied elevation, and uses a six-story tower as its centerpiece. The complex acts as a southern bookend to the campus, while Burges' work is the bookend to the north.

Defined by these residence halls, Summit Court is a man-made plateau that defines and engages a corner of the Life Sciences Quadrangle. A 12-foot-wide ramp (with occasional steps) acts as a medieval street entering an Italian hill town, leading to the Summit Tower and creating an almost seamless connection between the Summit Court and the larger quad below.

The Summit Tower announces the presence of the college when viewed from the south. In addition, the tower refers to the College's Chapel Tower, the iconic image farther to the north. The Summit Tower's form is deliberately non-historic—forming the head to a linear building without resorting to traditional gable or pyramided tower forms. It also signals the importance of the Residence Hall Complex to the campus.

The buildings are organized into three residence halls—two halls in the bar building, one in Summit Tower. Suites consist of a living room, four single bedrooms, and a private bathroom. In two of the halls, a two-story common room, located on the second floor and accessible from the third floor, acts as the "heart of the hall." The Summit Tower includes a dining facility that can serve all the students in one hall at a time.

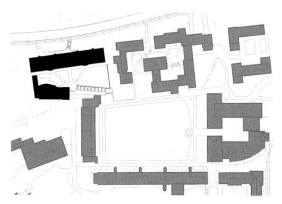

Site Plan

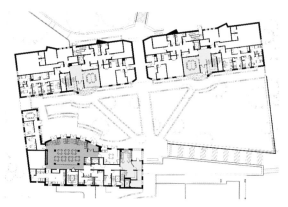

Ground Floor Plan

Curved façades help define the
intimate scale of the quad (above, left).
Two-story common rooms are located
on the second and third floors of
two halls, representing the central
element in each building (above, right).
Standing tall, the Summit Tower
asserts the college's presence when
viewed from the south (facing page).

Second Floor Plan

Credits

Charlestown Navy Yard Rowhouses
Boston, Massachusetts
CLIENT: Bricklayers and Laborers Non-Profit Housing Company, Inc.: Thomas McIntyre, Joanne Troy ARCHITECT: William Rawn Associates, Architects, Inc.: William L. Rawn III, FAIA, Principal for Design; Donald Klema, Associate; Jim Loman; Elizabeth Mahon LANDSCAPE ARCHITECT: Michael Van Valkenburgh Assoc., Inc. MECHANICAL ENGINEER: C.A. Crowley Engineering, Inc. STRUCTURAL ENGINEER: LeMessurier Consultants GENERAL CONTRACTOR: Mirabassi Associates PHOTOGRAPHER: Steve Rosenthal

Columbus Fire Station No.6
Columbus, Indiana
CLIENT: City of Columbus, Columbus Fire Department: Fred Armstrong, Mayor; Gary Burriss, Fire Chief ARCHITECTURAL SPONSOR: Cummins Engine Foundation ARCHITECT: William Rawn Associates, Architects, Inc.: William L. Rawn III, FAIA, Principal for Design; Alan Joslin, AIA, Senior Associate/Project Architect; Christopher Kenney, Project Manager; Matthew Cohen; Reinerio Faife LANDSCAPE ARCHITECT: Jack Curtis & Associates LIGHTING CONSULTANT: Ripman Lighting Consultants MECHANICAL ENGINEER: TMP Consulting Engineers, Inc. STRUCTURAL ENGINEER: LeMessurier Consultants GENERAL CONTRACTOR: Dunlap & Company PHOTOGRAPHER: Balthazar Korab

Exeter Music Building
Exeter, New Hampshire
CLIENT: Phillips Exeter Academy: Kendra O'Donnell, Principal DESIGN COMMITTEE: Kendra O'Donnell, Steven Kushner, Don Briselden, Lynda Beck, Mimi Bravar, James Rogers, Ilona Weber ARCHITECT: William Rawn Associates, Architects, Inc.: William L. Rawn III, FAIA, Principal for Design; Alan Joslin, AIA, Senior Associate/Project Architect; Randy Wilmot, Job Captain; Steven Hart; Richard Yeager; Sean Wang; Lindsay Crawford; David Yosick; Katie Hutchison; Brian LaBau; Robert Linn; Nicole Bouvier ACOUSTICIAN: Kirkegaard Associates LANDSCAPE ARCHITECT: Michael Van Valkenburgh Assoc., Inc. LIGHTING CONSULTANT: Ripman Lighting Consultants MECHANICAL ENGINEER: TMP Consulting Engineers, Inc. STRUCTURAL ENGINEER: LeMessurier Consultants GENERAL CONTRACTOR: Hutter Construction Company PHOTOGRAPHER: Steve Rosenthal

Glavin Family Chapel
Wellesley, Massachusetts
CLIENT: Babson College: William Glavin, President DESIGN COMMITTEE: Cecily Glavin, David Carson, Fred Muzi, John McQuillen, Janet Sanders, Sister Frances M. Sheehey, Richard Snyder, Michael Veneto ARCHITECT: William Rawn Associates, Architects, Inc.: William L. Rawn III, FAIA, Principal for Design; Alan Joslin, AIA, Senior Associate/Project Architect; Robert Wear, Project Manager; Robert Linn, Job Captain; Matthew Cohen; Robert Linn; Mark Johnson; Sean Wang ACOUSTICIAN: Kirkegaard Associates LANDSCAPE ARCHITECT: Carol R. Johnson Associates LIGHTING CONSULTANT: Ripman Lighting Consultants MECHANICAL ENGINEER: TMP Consulting Engineers, Inc. STRUCTURAL ENGINEER: LeMessurier Consultants ALTAR & DOORS: Rick Wrigley, Gatehouse Furnishings HANGING HULL FABRICATOR: Mitch Ryerson with Rick Wrigley STAINED GLASS ARTIST: Peter McGrain STAINED GLASS FABRICATOR: Serpentino Glass TOWER SCULPTURE: Frances G. Pratt GENERAL CONTRACTOR: Erland Construction PHOTOGRAPHER: Steve Rosenthal

Donald and Maureen Green Music Center
Sonoma, California
CLIENT: Sonoma State University: Ruben Armiñana, President DESIGN COMMITTEE: Floyd Ross, Marne Olson, Larry Furukawa-Schlereth, Jeff Langley, Bob Worth, John Bond, Bruce Walker, Deborah DuVall DESIGN ARCHITECT: William Rawn Associates, Architects, Inc.: William L. Rawn III, FAIA and Alan Joslin, AIA, Principals for Design; Vinicius Gorgati, Associate/Project Architect; Philip Gray; Peter Reiss; Laura Bouwman; John Paul Guerrero; Sarah Michelman EXECUTIVE ARCHITECT: AC Martin Partners, Inc. ACOUSTICIAN: Kirkegaard Associates THEATER

CONSULTANT: Auerbach + Associates LANDSCAPE ARCHITECT: Quadriga MECHANICAL ENGINEER: Ove Arup & Partners STRUCTURAL ENGINEER: Ove Arup & Partners RENDERING: Al Forester

Institute of Contemporary Art
Boston, Massachusetts
CLIENT: Institute of Contemporary Art: David Ross, Director (1989), Malina Kalinovska, Director (1992) ARCHITECT: William Rawn Associates, Architects, Inc.: William L. Rawn III, FAIA, Principal for Design; Clifford V. Gayley, AIA, Senior Associate/Project Architect; Robert Genova; Rick Jones; Lola Vogt PHOTOGRAPHER: Steve Rosenthal (model) RENDERING: Don Paine

Loews Boston Hotel
Boston, Massachusetts
CLIENTS: Sawyer Enterprises: Carol Parks, John Connolly; Loews Hotels: Jonathan M. Tisch, President; Jack S. Adler, Julie Purnell, Sherrie Laveronie, Michael Ferrera ARCHITECT: William Rawn Associates, Architects, Inc.: William L. Rawn III, FAIA, Principal for Design; Clifford V. Gayley, AIA, Associate Principal for Design/Project Architect; Sam Lasky, Project Architect; Mark Warner, Associate/Project Architect; Philip Gray, Project Manager; Adam Yang; Borislav Ignatov; Karl Anderson; Peter Reiss; Bailey Heck; Christopher Kenney; Kevin Bergeron; David Grissino; Matthew Stymiest; John Paul Guerrero; Frank Valdes; Eun-Sang Jeong; Deborah Marai ARCHITECT OF RECORD: Jung/Brannen Associates, Inc. CLADDING: Heitmann & Associates, Inc. GEOTECHNICAL ENGINEER: GZA Geoenvironmental HOTEL CONSULTANT: Horwath Landauer Hospitality Consulting, Inc. INTERIOR DESIGN: Aero Studios Ltd. LIGHTING CONSULTANT: Johnson Schwinghammer Lighting Consultants, Inc. MECHANICAL ENGINEER: TMP Consulting Engineers, Inc. PROJECT MANAGEMENT: Spaulding & Slye Colliers International, John L. Myers REGULATORY PROCESS: Mitchell Consultants: Bart Mitchell; Epsilon Associates, Inc: Cindy Schlessinger, Wil Donham; The Strategy Group: Susan Tracy, David Newman STRUCTURAL ENGINEER: LeMessurier Consultants CONSTRUCTION MANAGER: Turner Construction Company RENDERINGS: Frank M. Costantino (p.100); Neoscape (p.96-97)

The Pavilion at Symphony Lake
Cary, North Carolina
CLIENT: Town of Cary/North Carolina Symphony: Koka Booth, Mayor DESIGN COMMITTEE: Mary Barry, Director; Lyman Collins, David Brooks, Richard Burton, Glen Lang, Jack Smith, Melba Sparrow, Jess Ward, William B. Coleman, Alice Webb, Sam Bishop, Kay Stuffalino, Hyram Black ARCHITECT: William Rawn Associates, Architects, Inc.: Alan Joslin, AIA and William L. Rawn III, FAIA, Principals for Design; John Upton, Associate/ Project Manager; Gary Gwon, Project Architect for Pavilion; Ken Amano; Matthew Cohen; David Grissino; Victor Liu; Basil Richardson; Ryan Senkier ACOUSTICIAN: Kirkegaard Associates THEATER CONSULTANT: Theatre Projects Consultants LANDSCAPE ARCHITECT: Reynolds & Jewell LIGHTING CONSULTANT: Ripman Lighting Consultants MECHANICAL ENGINEER: TMP Consulting Engineers, Inc. STRUCTURAL ENGINEER: LeMessurier Consultants GENERAL CONTRACTOR: Barnhill Contracting Company PHOTOGRAPHER: Michael Zirkle

Rochester Riverfront Development
Rochester, New York
Rochester Riverfront Zoning Guidelines
CLIENT: City of Rochester: Thomas P. Ryan, Jr., Mayor; Christopher Lindley, Deputy Mayor; Fashun Ku ARCHITECT: William Rawn Associates, Architects, Inc.: William L. Rawn III, FAIA, Principal for Design; Douglas C. Johnston, AIA, Senior Associate/Project Architect; Ed McDonald; Richard Yeager
Main Public Library
CLIENT: Rochester Public Library: Richard Panz, Director; Jack R. Bowman, Chair of Committee; Rod Perry; Angelo Chiarella; Fashun Ku DESIGN ARCHITECT: William Rawn Associates, Architects, Inc.: William L. Rawn III, FAIA, Principal for Design; Clifford V. Gayley, AIA, Senior Associate/Project Architect; Robert Linn, Project Team ARCHITECT OF RECORD: LaBella Associates, P.C. INTERIOR DESIGN: Hafner Associates MECHANICAL ENGINEER: M/E Engineering, P.C. CONSTRUCTION MANAGER: Christa Construction,

William S. Carleton PHOTOGRAPHER: David Lamb

High Falls Garage

CLIENT: City of Rochester: Thomas P. Ryan, Jr., Mayor; Christopher Lindley, Deputy Mayor; Fashun Ku; Nancy H. Burton DESIGN ARCHITECT: William Rawn Associates, Architects, Inc.: William L. Rawn III, FAIA, Principal for Design; Clifford V. Gayley, AIA, Senior Associate/ Project Architect; Richard Yeager; David Yosick; Laura Yanchencko; Amy Klee; Nicole Bouvier; Jennifer Schank ARCHITECT OF RECORD: LaBella Associates, P.C. LIGHTING CONSULTANT: Stone Mountain Lasers, Inc. MECHANICAL ENGINEER: Robson & Woese, Inc. Consulting Engineers PARKING CONSULTANT: Carl Walker Engineers GENERAL CONTRACTOR: Christa Construction PHOTOGRAPHER: David Lamb

Sister Cities Garage

CLIENT: City of Rochester: Thomas P. Ryan, Jr., Mayor; Fashun Ku; Suressa H. Forbes; Nancy H. Burton DESIGN ARCHITECT: William Rawn Associates, Architects, Inc.: William L. Rawn III, FAIA, Principal for Design; Douglas C. Johnston, AIA, Senior Associate/Project Architect; Renee Cheng ARCHITECT OF RECORD: QPK Architects CONSTRUCTION MANAGER: Raymond LeChase PHOTOGRAPHER: David Lamb

Seiji Ozawa Hall at Tanglewood
Lenox, Massachusetts

CLIENT: Boston Symphony Orchestra: George Kidder, President DESIGN COMMITTEE: Dean Freed, Daniel R. Gustin, Haskell Gordon, Robert Campbell ARCHITECT: William Rawn Associates, Architects, Inc.: William L. Rawn III, FAIA, Principal for Design; Alan Joslin, AIA, Senior Associate/Project Architect; Clifford V. Gayley, AIA, Associate/Job Captain; Cressler Heasley; Jack Robbins; Tomas Rossant; Laura Yanchenko; Richard Yeager; David Yosick; Elizabeth Zachos ACOUSTICIAN: Kirkegaard Associates THEATER CONSULTANT: Theatre Projects Consultants COST CONSULTANT: Donnell Consultants, Inc. LANDSCAPE ARCHITECT: Michael Van Valkenburgh Assoc., Inc. LIGHTING CONSULTANT: Douglas Baker MECHANICAL ENGINEER: TMP Consulting Engineers, Inc. STRUCTURAL ENGINEER: LeMessurier Consultants CONTRACTOR: Suffolk Construction Company, Inc. PHOTOGRAPHERS: Steve Rosenthal (p.20-21); Walter Scott (p.24)

The Summit Residence Complex and Court
Hartford, Connecticut

CLIENT: Trinity College: Evan S. Dobelle, President; Michael West; Ronald W. Thomas; John Wooley; Alden Gordon; Jim Mullin ARCHITECT: William Rawn Associates, Architects, Inc.: William L. Rawn III, FAIA and Alan Joslin, AIA, Principals for Design; Randy Wilmot, Associate/Project Manager; Hank Scollard; Lisa Giovanetti; Basil Richardson; Laura Gilmore; Wei-Chung Chang; Jessica Stander; Denise Ferris; Robin Sakahara; Christine Everett; Christian Dick; Matt Gindel LANDSCAPE ARCHITECT: Andropogon Associates LIGHTING CONSULTANT: Ripman Lighting Consultants MECHANICAL ENGINEER: Van Zelm Heywood & Shadford, Inc. STRUCTURAL ENGINEER: LeMessurier Consultants GENERAL CONTRACTOR: Gilbane Building Company PHOTOGRAPHER: Steve Rosenthal

Strathmore Concert Hall
Montgomery County, Maryland

CLIENTS: State of Maryland: Parris Glendening, Governor, Montgomery County, Maryland; Douglas Duncan, County Executive; Al Roshdieh; Mary K. Donahoe STRATHMORE HALL DESIGN COMMITTEE: Charles Lyons, Eliot Pfanstiehl, John Gidwitz, Mario Loiederman, Alan Mowbray, David Phillips DESIGN ARCHITECT: William Rawn Associates, Architects, Inc.: William L. Rawn III, FAIA and Alan Joslin, AIA, Principals for Design; Jeanne A. Kuespert, Associate/Project Manager; Gary Gwon, Project Architect; Clifford V. Gayley, AIA, Associate Principal; Philip Gray, Associate/Technical Director; Vinicius Gorgati, Associate; Euiseok Jeong; Frank Valdes; David Bagnoli; Miguel Rionda; Victor Liu; Jose Soliva; Stan Gasasira; Daniel Martell; Wei-Chung Chang; Christian Dick; Eri Ishida ASSOCIATED ARCHITECT: Grimm and Parker Architects: Stephen Parker, President; Sue Hains, Project Manager ACOUSTICIAN: Kirkegaard Associates THEATER CONSULTANT: Theatre Projects Consultants

COST CONSULTANT: Donnell Consultants, Inc. LANDSCAPE ARCHITECTS: Louise Schiller Associates, with LDR International LANDSCAPE CONSULTANT: Fisher Marantz Stone, Inc. MECHANICAL ENGINEER: TMP Consulting Engineers, Inc. PROJECT MANAGEMENT: Tishman Construction Corporation, Inc. STRUCTURAL ENGINEER: LeMessurier Consultants RENDERING: Frank M. Costantino

Superblock Housing Competition
Philadelphia, Pennsylvania

CLIENT: University of Pennsylvania: Judith Rodin, President ARCHITECT: William Rawn Associates, Architects, Inc.: William L. Rawn III, FAIA, Principal for Design; Clifford V. Gayley, AIA, Associate Principal for Design/Project Architect; Euiseok Jeong; Basil Richardson; Neil Walls; Wei-Chung Chang; Jared Craft; Timothy Campbell; Christian Dick PHOTOGRAPHER: Steve Rosenthal (model)

West Campus Residence Halls
Boston, Massachusetts

CLIENT: Northeastern University: Richard Freeland, President; Jack Martin, Vice President; Larry Mucciolo, Executive Vice President; Dan Bourque; Nancy May; Jack Malone; Ed Duffy ARCHITECT: William Rawn Associates, Architects, Inc.: William L. Rawn III, FAIA, Principal for Design; Clifford V. Gayley, AIA, Associate Principal for Design/Project Architect; Christopher Kenney, Associate/Project Manager (Phase I); Anne-Sophie Divenyi, Project Manager (Phase II); Rob Wear, Associate/Senior Architect (Phases I, II); Kevin Bergeron, Job Captain (Phase I); Lindsay Crawford, Job Captain for Exterior (Phases I, II); Sam Lasky, Job Captain for Curtain Wall (Phase II); Neil Walls, Job Captain for Interior (Phases I, II); Jessica Anderson; Tony Antonja; Lisa Bonfiglio; Daniel Burhans; Wei-Chung Chang; John Clegg; Christian Dick; Denise Ferris; Jennifer Garceau; Rob Genova; Matt Gindel; Lisa Giovanetti; Gary Gwon; Julie Thomas Hess; Alison Kopyt; Victor Liu; Brad Lucas; Deborah Marai; Ed Maximo; Jack Melvin; Jennifer Neuwalder; Michael O'Keefe; Jonathan Parker; Robin Sakahara; Christian Schaller; John Upton; Kristina Vardaro; Lola Vogt; Peter Wells; Hannah Whipple; Ke Zhang; and Douglas C. Johnston, AIA, Principal (Master Plan) GEOTECHNICAL ENGINEER: Haley & Aldrich, Inc. LANDSCAPE ARCHITECT: Pressley Associates, Inc. LIGHTING CONSULTANT: Ripman Lighting Consultants MECHANICAL ENGINEER: TMP Consulting Engineers, Inc. STRUCTURAL ENGINEER: LeMessurier Consultants CONSTRUCTION MANAGER: Turner Construction Company PHOTOGRAPHER: Steve Rosenthal

West Main Street Corridor Urban Design Plan
Charlottesville, Virginia

CLIENTS: University of Virginia: John Casteen, President; Leonard Sandridge; Tim Rose; Jules I. Levine; Harry Porter; City of Charlottesville: David Toscano, Kay Slaughter, Gary O'Connell, Eugene Williams ARCHITECT: William Rawn Associates, Architects, Inc.: William L. Rawn III, FAIA, Principal for Design; Clifford V. Gayley, AIA, Senior Associate/Project Architect; Craig Mutter; Ed McDonald; Richard Yeager COLLABORATING ARCHITECTS: Hanbury Evans Newill Vlattas & Co., Metcalf Tobey Davis RENDERING: Wesley Page (p.121) PHOTOGRAPHER: William Rawn

Essay Photography Credits:
A ROOM FOR MUSIC p.10-11: William Rawn; #1-6: William Rawn; #7-9: Walter Scott; #10-11: Steve Rosenthal; #12: Paul Warchol; p.16-17: Walter Scott; #13: Steve Rosenthal; #14: Paul Warchol; #15: Walter Scott; p.19: Steve Rosenthal WHERE THE CITY MEETS THE WATER p.60-61 William Rawn; #16 Alex S. MacLean/Landslides; #17: Alex S. MacLean/Landslides; #18-22: William Rawn; #23, 24: Steve Rosenthal; #25-27: William Rawn; p.66-67: Michael Zirkle; #28, 29: William Rawn; #30: Steve Rosenthal; p.69: Steve Rosenthal CAMPUS AND THE CITY p.102-103: William Rawn; #31: Alex S. MacLean/Landslides; #32-34:William Rawn; #35: Alex S. MacLean/Landslides; #36-42: William Rawn; p.108-109: Alex S. MacLean/Landslides; #43, 44: Alex S. MacLean/Landslides; #45-48: Steve Rosenthal; p.144: Joe Greene

Acknowledgements
by William Rawn

The path to architecture is rarely a simple one; my route was perhaps particularly indirect. Looking back, I see that generous-spirited friends and loyal colleagues influenced my most important choices—they warrant acknowledgement.

I would like to thank Yale College and Vincent Scully for giving architecture the intellectual credibility that surprisingly recharged a deep childhood interest; Harold Roth, whose passion for architecture convinced me to try it myself at the age of 30; Imre Halasz at MIT, who personified the generosity of the university teacher; and two friends from Barcelona, Miguel Corominas and Joaquim Sabate, who exposed me, the American student, to contemporary European architecture at a particularly powerful moment in my life.

If I have had three distinct careers—law, university administration, and architecture—I have had only three jobs and three mentors. My thanks go to Harry Plotkin and Robert Wood for their mentorship in the first two "careers," and to Lewis Davis, whose ethical commitment to the city and to his employees influenced me more than he will ever know. I have known no model of practice other than his. I would also like to thank the Pace Gallery, for its decade-long support of my artwork, which ironically gave me the confidence to pursue architecture.

I must acknowledge Boston, a city that so deeply supports the role of the architect in its core culture, a city which sets a premium on meritocracy and which welcomes thousands of outsiders who come to study and then decide to stay. Boston's quality of urban life is at once embracing and demanding, the perfect combination for success in architecture.

The buildings in this book would not have been possible without my professional colleagues in the firm, from the first employee in 1983 to the 55 today: their collaboration has been fundamental to our success. Particular thanks goes to Alan Joslin, Doug Johnston, and Cliff Gayley for their leadership over the past decades, and to those who have worked with us in the past and those who will join us over the coming years.

Architecture is inspired and strengthened by intense dialogue with clients. Their clarity of vision, intellectual curiosity, and humane patience nourished has our work on every project. Special acknowledgment goes to those clients who hired us for a building type we had never done before—exhibiting a confidence which expanded our minds, our ken. And two colleagues who have worked closely with us from the very beginning deserve special mention: Steve Rosenthal, a photographer with an extraordinary eye and gentle spirit; and LeMessurier Consultants, a structural engineering firm of remarkable intelligence and genuine teamwork.

Most importantly, my close friends and family encouraged me to take the initial big steps toward architecture, and through three decades supported me through its inevitable passion and preoccupation. They sustained me on this journey in ways I cannot express.

Architecture is a "patient search." As Le Corbusier observed, it is a search that is intellectually enriching, forever challenging, and ultimately rewarding in its permanence. To the field, for what it has always been and always will be, I offer my ultimate thanks.

Left to Right: Douglas Johnston, William Rawn, Clifford Gayley

Selected Projects

National AIA Honor Awards:

Seiji Ozawa Hall at Tanglewood
Lenox, Massachusetts
1995 AIA HONOR AWARD IN ARCHITECTURE

Charlestown Navy Yard Rowhouses
Bricklayers and Laborers Non-Profit
Housing Co., Inc.
Boston, Massachusetts
1994 AIA HONOR AWARD IN ARCHITECTURE

1995 LOUIS SULLIVAN AWARD FOR ARCHITECTURE

Seiji Ozawa Hall at Tanglewood
Lenox, Massachusetts
2000 AIA HONOR AWARD IN INTERIORS

Back of the Hill Rowhouses
Bricklayers and Laborers Non-Profit
Housing Co., Inc.
Boston, Massachusetts
**1993 URBAN DESIGN AWARD OF EXCELLENCE
(FORERUNNER TO AIA HONOR AWARD)**

University of Virginia/City of Charlottesville
West Main Street Urban Design Plan [1]
Charlottesville, Virginia
1996 AIA HONOR AWARD IN URBAN DESIGN

Village of Park DuValle [2]
Community Builders Inc.
Louisville, Kentucky
2000 AIA HONOR AWARD IN URBAN DESIGN

DreamWorks SKG, Corporate
Headquarters and Production
Studios Conceptual Design [3]
Los Angeles, California

Strathmore Concert Hall [4]
Montgomery County (Owner)
Montgomery County, Maryland

University of Virginia Arts
Precinct Conceptual Design [5]
Charlottesville, Virginia

Lawrenceville School
Music Building
Lawrenceville, New Jersey

Trinity College Residence Halls
Hartford, Connecticut

Grinnell College Residence Halls
Grinnell, Iowa

Josie Robertson Plaza Design
Lincoln Center for the
Performing Arts
New York, New York

Keene State College
Campus Center
Keene, New Hampshire

Bowdoin College Residence Hall
Brunswick, Maine

Amherst College Residence Hall
Amherst, Massachusetts

Phillips Exeter Academy
Forrestal-Bowld Music Building
Exeter, New Hampshire

Bates College Residential Village
Lewiston, Maine

Miami University
Center for the Arts [6]
Oxford, Ohio

San Diego Housing Block [7]
San Diego, California

Institute of Contemporary Art
Boston, Massachusetts

The Pavilion at Symphony Lake
Town of Cary
Cary, North Carolina

Fire Station No. 6
Columbus, Indiana

Rochester Public Library (Main
Library) [8]
Sister Cities Parking Garage [9]
High Falls Parking Garage [10]
City of Rochester
Rochester, New York

Green Music Center [11]
Sonoma State University
Sonoma County, California

Lowell Performance Pavilion [12]
National Park Service
Lowell, Massachusetts

Dartmouth College
Downtown Housing
and Retail
Hanover, New Hampshire

Dartmouth College
Faculty Housing
Hanover, New Hampshire

Swarthmore College
Residence Halls
Swarthmore, Pennsylvania

Gordon College Music Building
Wenham, Massachusetts

College of William
and Mary, Lake Matoaka
Amphitheater
Williamsburg, Virginia

Pine Manor College
Campus Center
Chestnut Hill, Massachusetts

Williams College Center for
Theatre and Dance
Williamstown, Massachusetts

Accord Norwell Office Park
Norwell, Massachusetts

Northeastern University
Residence Halls
Boston, Massachusetts

Northeastern University
Computer Science
Building & Residence Hall
Boston, Massachusetts

Northeastern University
Master Plan
Boston, Massachusetts

Church of the Transfiguration
Community of Jesus
Orleans, Massachusetts

Community Performing Arts
Center [13]
Seaside, Florida

Milton Academy Campus
Crossroads [14]
Milton, Massachusetts

Babson College Campus Center
Babson College Theater
Babson College Chapel
Wellesley, Massachusetts

Carneros Inn Resort [15]
Carneros Partners
Napa Valley, California

Yale University Campus
Police Station
New Haven, Connecticut

Battle Road Farm (Housing)
Keen Development Corporation
Lincoln, Massachusetts

Cleveland Plain Dealer
Headquarters Competition
Cleveland, Ohio

United States Federal
Courthouse Competition
Springfield, Massachusetts

Fort Trumbull Hotel and Housing
Corcoran Jennison Inc.
New London, Connecticut

Loews Boston Hotel [16]
Sawyer Enterprises
Boston, Massachusetts

Walt Disney Company
Celebration School and
Teaching Academy [17]
Celebration, Florida

Cambridge Public Library
(Main Library) [18]
Cambridge, Massachusetts

Associated Architectural Firms:
**(1) Hanbury Evans Newill Vlattas &
Co.; Metcalf Tobey Davis**
**(2) Urban Design Associates; Stull &
Lee; Tucker & Booker Inc.**
(3) Gensler
(4) Grimm + Parker Architects
(5) Glave & Holmes Associates
(6) Lorenz + Williams
(7) Tucker, Sadler & Associates
(8) LaBella Associates
**(9) Quinlivan Pierik & Krause,
Architects/Engineers**
(10) LaBella Associates
(11) AC Martin Partners, Inc.
(12) Brown and Rowe
(13) DAG Architects, Inc.
**(14) Finegold Alexander +
Associates Inc.**
(15) RMW Architecture
(16) Jung/Brannen & Associates
**(17) Schenkel Schultz; KBJ
Architects**
(18) Ann Beha Architects